Why I Believe

Mark Joseph Young

©2020 Mark Joseph Young
ISBN: 978-1-989940-09-9
Dimensionfold Publishing

Cover photo by Aaron Burden on Unsplash

To my father,
who taught me the basics of rational thought;

and to L. Grey "Hot" Vanaman,
who perhaps unintentionally motivated the creation
of this book.

Why I Believe

Somewhere Neil deGrasse Tyson has said that it is a significant point that when you reach the top, the most brilliant scientific minds in the world, there is still a significant percentage of them who believe in God.

He did not have me in mind. However, I am one of those smart people who believe, and people are surprised at that and find it difficult to grasp. One friend of mine who happens to be a lapsed Baptist has specifically commented that I am the smartest person he knows (his assessment) and the fact that I am a believer is a problem for his unbelief. It is generally thought, and particularly by people of modestly above average intelligence, that if you are smart enough you won't believe in God, because God is not more than an explanation for that which we do not understand. The attitude is pervasive enough that some Christians (misreading the points of I Corinthians 1:26[1] and 3:19[2]) have claimed that intelligence is an obstacle to faith, almost that you have to be stupid to believe, and thus being stupid is an advantage. If this were so, then the intelligent would be quite justified in rejecting something which is nonsense on its face; but Christianity is not nonsense, but an entirely different kind of foolishness, a kind of foolishness which makes perfect sense once you understand it.[3] So maybe

---

[1] To the effect that there are not many wise among Christians, which only means that the wise, noble, and wealthy are not found in greater percentage in the church than in the world.

[2] To the effect that the wisdom of the world is foolishness to God, see next note.

[3] It is the foolishness of placing the interests and needs of others above those of yourself, instead of working to advance

there's a sense in which if you are smart enough you will believe.

A friend of mine[4] has conjectured that were we to create superintelligent artificial intelligences, they would become believers, because they would be forced to that conclusion by their own logic. He thinks that no one fails to believe in God because of anything other than the wish to be the masters of their own destinies. I don't know that I agree. I don't know that the logic of the situation is *compelling*. Yet I think that the preponderance of the evidence favors the existence not only of God but of the Christian message as the ultimate truth about God—possibly to the level of clear and convincing, if we are using legal terminology for levels of proof.

It seems to me, though, that for any of this to have any meaning, you would have to accept that I am intelligent. It is easy enough to say of anyone that he must not be all that intelligent if he believes in God—just as one might say that of someone who believes in leprechauns or ghosts or the inherent beneficence of all humanity. Liberal Democrats make the claim of conservative Republicans, and conservative Republicans of liberal Democrats that they are not very intelligent and fail to understand simple logic.[5] Even some who have met me perhaps question my intellectual prowess, and I have the greatest of respect for them. I grew up thinking I was of average intellect, and did not know that I was

---

yourself at the expense of others.

[4] Eric R. Ashley, author of several books and innumerable online articles. He has since called my attention to a book in which artificially intelligent machines believe in God.

[5] The problem here is not intelligence but values, that we disagree concerning what the important things are.

"smarter than the average bear" until I was a quarter of a century old and held two (undergraduate) college degrees. The only person who ever told me I was intelligent, as far as I remember, was my mother, and she also told me I was handsome, so I knew she was lying. After all, wouldn't someone who was intelligent and handsome also be popular?[6] If the fact that my opinion as a "superintelligent" person is going to matter to you, you have to believe that I am in fact such a person; and that puts me in the awkward position of having to brag about a few things that to me seem quite ordinary yet are apparently unusual.

The summer of 1986, when I turned thirty-one, I often say was the most fun I'd had in a number of years, because I got to take a lot of tests and I did well at them. I was in one of those times when the future was murky, and it seemed that continuing my education was the best course, but there was no obvious direction for that. Thus I took several tests to determine my options. I will give you this advice, which may help you in any academic or scholastic or similar tests you face. Tests are merely games, and if you go into them thinking of them as games and relax and enjoy playing, you will perform better. What makes people nervous is not the game but the stakes, that somehow we think our entire life hangs on how we perform on this test. Whether or not that's true, you will perform better if you ignore the

---

[6] In fairness to my father, I cannot say he never told me I was intelligent, but I can say that he always treated me as if I were. Of course, not having had any other father, I did not have any basis for comparison; and when I became a father and at times a surrogate father to the children of others, I always treated them as if they were intelligent, so it is more an indication of parenting style than of specific belief about the child.

stakes and play the game. So I had fun playing the game of four tests, because the outcomes only mattered in that I needed to see how well (or poorly) I did. My future did in one sense hinge on the outcome, but it was not a matter of the future I wanted to pursue requiring me to succeed, but that my level of success would determine what futures I might pursue.

The first of the four tests was actually two tests, the Mensa qualifying tests, high-level intelligence quotient (I.Q.) tests designed to determine if a candidate is in the top two percent of the population by intelligence—the ninety-eighth percentile. That sounds impressive, but as I said to my brother Roy, it's only one in fifty, and if of a hundred randomly selected people in a room you would be one of the two smartest, you qualify. Also, you only have to qualify on one of the tests. I qualified on both; in fact, I scored the ninety-ninth percentile on each, which means that of that random hundred people I am probably the smartest.

O.K., many people are underwhelmed by I.Q. testing, and I accept that. The second test I took was the Armed Services Vocational Aptitude Battery (A.S.V.A.B.). This is a nine-section test, although the first section, General Science, is generally believed to be there to orient the candidate to the test system and only matters in that you are expected to complete it. Tests two through five cover mathematics and language skills and are considered the intelligence portion of the test; six through nine are technical and considered the vocational portion, testing mostly how much background you already have in various technologies. Although I never saw all the scores (the recruiter seemed to want to downplay my results and talk me into a minor position in the local reserves) the test administrator informed me that I had every question correct on the intelligence portion.

In June I took the Graduate Records Examinations (G.R.E.). This test is scored on the same 200 to 800 scale as the Scholastic Aptitude Test (S.A.T.) administered by the same testing service, and is given exclusively to those who have completed or nearly completed an undergraduate college program and believe they are smart enough to continue into graduate school. On the verbal portion I scored 730; on the numerical, 710. That score surprised me, frankly, because it rated high (I do not now recall how high) as a percentile, and it meant that I did better in the math portion than most math, engineering, and science majors, despite having mostly avoided math classes in college and having not been a student for a decade. More significantly, though, this was the first time they included the Analytical portion. Some years later my wife told me she met someone smarter than I, reporting that his G.R.E. Analytical score was 790. I stared at her dumbstruck, because she somehow had not heard or not remembered that mine was, out of a possible 800, 800.

The jewel in the crown, though, is undoubtedly the Law School Admission Test (L.S.A.T.). This is an all-day test of reasoning ability, comprised of various types of logic problems—analogies, syllogisms[7], and puzzles. It is given again to those who have finished or nearly finished college and believe in this case that they are smart enough to continue in law school. At the time the score range

---

[7] "Arguments" (in the formal sense).

was ten to forty-eight; my score was forty-eight. According to the materials that were sent with the score, a forty-eight on that test placed me in the top one fifth of one percent of people who were already persuaded that they were intelligent enough for law school and had at least some evidence to support that belief in the form of scholastic achievement.

So if I'm so smart, why aren't I rich, or at least famous? Well, I doubt whether very many of those people on Neil DeGrasse Tyson's list of the smartest scientists in the world are either rich or, outside their fields, famous. I am known world-wide as the co-author of the Multiverser role playing game and a role playing game theory writer (some of my work has been translated into German and French and republished), the chaplain of the Christian Gamers Guild, and perhaps the leading proponent of the "replacement theory" of time travel, but even within those fields I'm not one of the big names. That's partly because I am a generalist; specialists tend to excel.[8] It is also because I've never been good at selling anything, least of all myself. But ultimately it is because intelligence is not really one of the most marketable skills. It does not make one a good salesman or a good organizer or administrator. It is mostly useful for identifying and analyzing problems, working through theoretical problems and devising solutions or new applications, and for teaching. In any case, what matters is that you accept that my claim to intelligence is not simply some blowhard bragging, but is supported by

---

[8] A generalist is someone who learns less and less about more and more until eventually he knows nothing about everything, while a specialist conversely learns more and more about less and less until he knows everything about nothing.

something in reality. By the end of the book you will probably have come to your own conclusion regarding whether or not I am intelligent; it is of no consequence to me what you conclude; what matters is whether upon reaching the end you understand that intelligent people can believe in God. To get there, I ask that you give me the benefit of the doubt initially.

Some will no doubt notice the frequency with which I cite C. S. Lewis, and suppose that my position is derived from his. He is not the only person I cite, but he is the one (outside the Bible) whom I cite most frequently.[9] Two things must be said in reply to this.

The first is that C. S. Lewis was unquestionably the greatest popular apologist of the twentieth century, explaining and defending Christianity to more people than perhaps everyone else put together. He was a prolific writer who applied his considerable intellectual talents perhaps to every issue faced by Christians in the first half of that century (he died on the day John F. Kennedy was assassinated). It would not be intellectually credible for anyone to discuss the problem of pain or the viability of the miraculous without reference to his books on those subjects, for example. Further, whether or not he is always the best source on a given subject, he is generally the most accessible— his writing style is easy (I suspect far more so than mine) and he explains things clearly enough for the ordinary person to grasp, even when dealing with difficult theological matters.

---

[9] I use to joke that there was a new DSM-IV classification for people who frequently quote C. S. Lewis.

The second reply is that I had never heard of him until well after I was relatively established in my opinions. I had read many books on Christian life, but it was not until I was in college that I was introduced to his name.[10] I have since read scores of his books; he is undoubtedly my favorite author. My ability to articulate on these subjects is no doubt due in part to his influence, and he has undoubtedly contributed to the depth of my understanding. Yet this is because he is so often right and so often insightful and so often clear. You will find within these pages reference to William Paley, John Calvin, David Hume, Lee Strobel, John Wenham, Bruce Metzger, F. F. Bruce, and others, and I could mention scores of others. Lewis stands apart, in part because he covered the field so broadly[11] and in part because he is such an easy author to read. It is difficult to apologize for frequently citing the work of someone who said first what I wish I had said, better than I could have said it.

---

[10] Actually, when I was a junior in high school I was corresponding with a young girl with whom I was quite smitten who wrote about a series called *The Chronicles of Narnia*, but I dismissed it as fantasy nonsense until I encountered it myself two years later at college.

[11] Metzger, for example, is undoubtedly one of the best sources for the authenticity of the New Testament text, a subject on which Lewis rarely touched other than suggesting that there were people like Metzger working to assure that we had an authentic text; Metzger does not write much outside his area of expertise.

Objections

It is often suggested to me that I believe in Christianity for what C. S. Lewis would say were causes, not reasons. That is, I was raised in Christian churches in a Christian culture, and had I been raised in Saudi Arabia I would be Muslim, or in India I would be Hindu or Buddhist. Or I am told that I embrace Christianity because of my own insecurities.

The first response to this is that on one level it is immaterial. That is, if my belief is caused by my background rather than chosen by my intellect, that does not make what I believe untrue. You cannot dismiss what I believe simply by assigning a causal explanation for the belief; you have to assess whether the belief itself has merit apart from that cause. That further means that even if it were demonstrated that I believed because—causally—I was taught to believe, it would still require an assessment of whether I believe because—logically —the evidence supports it. For example, I believe that the earth is round, the sun is roughly eight light minutes away, and the planets, including the earth, revolve around the sun. The cause of that belief is that I was raised to believe it. I have since investigated the reasons for that belief and found them sufficient. If I have also investigated the reasons for my belief in God, and in Jesus Christ as God, and found the reasons sufficient, the initial cause of that belief is irrelevant.

It is also doubtful. It is true that my parents considered themselves to be Christians[12] and took me to church from as early as I can recall (American Baptist Convention in the earliest years, later United Presbyterian Church). However, part of their reason for selecting the Baptist church (as opposed to, say, the Methodists or Presbyterians) is that the Baptists do not baptize infants and thus do not presume to tell you that you are a member of their faith, a believer, until you make that decision independently.[13]   I was thus presented with the contents of the Bible from a very early age (as a preschooler I studied *The Golden Book of Bible Stories*), but I was never pressured to become a Christian. In the main, my mother wanted me to reach my own conclusions concerning what I believed. She interfered once, when I was twelve

---

[12] The definitions of what it actually is to be "Christian" are numerous and often contradictory; without passing judgment either favorably or unfavorably, I prefer to identify others as claiming to be Christian. Thus the Pope claims to be Christian, as do the Mormons, the Baptists, the Lutherans, the Mennonites, the Quakers, the Jehovah's Witnesses, and many others, and while I might disagree with their definition and believe that their beliefs or practices are inconsistent with Christianity as I understand it, it is not my place to judge who is or is not Christian, only to explain my own understanding of the faith as well as I am able.

[13] It is also noteworthy in this regard that the concept of freedom of religion was created by the early Baptist theologian Thomas Helwys, who was jailed by King James for publishing his treasonous and heretical notion that the government could not dictate a man's beliefs. The fundamental point was that if there is only one mediator between God and man, Jesus Christ (as it says in Hebrews), then the King cannot usurp that position and tell a man how to approach God. That attitude that each individual must reach his own beliefs, his own faith, is central to Baptist theology.

and asked about being baptized. She was right to do so, as I knew nothing about baptism at the time but that members of my Sunday School class were being baptized and I was not, so at that time my reasons for joining the church would have been that I wanted to be part of the peer group. That mistake having been averted, she left me to reach my own conclusions. It is worth noting that I have three siblings, and they are not all believers, so if the supposed conditioning of my home life is the supposed cause of my belief, it did not prove terribly effective.

It is also significant that before I was thirteen we were no longer involved with the Baptists, due to having relocated to a town without an ecumenical Baptist church (ecumenism was an important factor to my parents). I was soon in a confirmation class in a Presbyterian church, studying the Bible with others my age who had been baptized as infants and were now going to confirm their faith. I did not join them in this, and for what is again a very telling reason: I felt that the classes had explained much about what it was to be Christian but nothing about what it was to be Presbyterian. I had some idea what Presbyterians believed, and knew that they did not agree entirely with Baptists, but wanted to know why I should be Presbyterian instead of, for example, Lutheran or Episcopalian (who were part of our ecumenical youth group program) or Catholic or Baptist (who were not). I wanted to know who was right before I made a commitment to a particular church. I had insufficient information, not even entirely certain what it meant to be a Presbyterian as opposed to any of these other groups. (I actually learned more at that time about what Presbyterians believed from a booklet on the subject published by the Roman Catholic Church; but then, I cannot really fault the Presbyterian church for not fully explaining its distinctives to young adults who had grown up in its Bible classes, as for most of them it would only confuse matters.)

It might be claimed that my decision to believe was driven by emotion, as perhaps happens to some who hear an impassioned evangelistic message, who for fear of hell or hope of joy come forward to receive Christ. Although I understand the skepticism toward such conversions, I think it misplaced; if the message reaches a buried need within the person, the conversion might well be highly emotional yet still be a rational response to a rational message. There is nothing irrational about grabbing a lifeline thrown to you when you are drowning, whatever emotion might drive the decision to do so. Mine, however, was not emotional. It was a quiet few minutes with a cousin, who using some printed material showed me in a very intellectual way that what I knew from the Bible was not some abstract conception of dogma but an invitation to a personal relationship with God. My decision was in that sense driven by reason, that this action is the logical conclusion of what I know.

I was thirteen at the time, and although I was more intelligent as a child than I knew I certainly could be faulted were I now to claim that having at that point reasoned through the matter I made the right decision and have stuck by it since. The fact is, there were good reasons then, and in the years since I have studied the matter in more detail and determined that there are other good reasons of which I was then completely unaware.

The Apologies

There are really two types of arguments for the existence of God, the one logical and the other empirical. There is some overlap between them, and perhaps the division is too simplistic. It may also be a bit irrelevant. What matters here is that there are arguments that have been propounded over the centuries. These had nothing to do with my initial decision to believe; on the other hand, I find that they support continued belief, and so they are worth discussing at least briefly.

At this point the discourse may seem a bit like a philosophy of religion text; for this I apologize. There is not much that can be done to reduce deep theological arguments to simple terms, but hopefully some of this will be successful. It is also necessary. It is surprising how many who claim that there is no evidence for the existence of God are completely unaware of any of these, and few know them all.

Ontology

When I was perhaps fourteen or fifteen, several
friends and I created "The Great Meditators
Society", which is probably a silly name for a silly
group of young teenagers trying to be intellectual.[14]
Our greatest discussion considered the fact that we
could not prove that the world around us existed,
that is, that what we thought we knew, even our
conversations with each other, were not completely
illusory. It might be, we concluded, that we exist as
a floating non-corporeal consciousness—that is, one
of us has such existence—and that there is some
other being who creates the illusion of a universe
and of interactions with other persons, giving us all
of our sensory information very like a dream.

If you want me to prove that God exists, it
cannot be done; I cannot even prove that you exist.
This we realized as teenagers. My experience is
better if I assume the illusion to be true, but a good
artificial intelligence driving a direct-to-mind virtual
reality   would   provide   the   same   outcome.
Cooperation with the rules of the illusion makes the
game more enjoyable, but this does not prove the
reality of the perceived world. (I should mention
that *The Matrix* would not exist for decades, and
was not part of our discussion.)

We of course were unaware that we were
rehashing intellectual ground much more ably
covered by others, particularly Rene Descartes. This
was the starting point for his major treatise, in which
he went beyond us to doubt his own existence, but

---

[14] Apart from myself, I recall the group including Paul Holland,
Rick Maus, and my brother Roy Young; Mike Nutry might
also have participated at one time or another.

then found a basis to believe that he, at least, existed in the one statement he made which is known by most people, "I think, therefore I am."[15] That then becomes the starting point for his own exposition of the ontological argument,[16] possibly the earliest and certainly the most basic of the formal arguments for the existence of God, propounded earlier by Athanasius.

I don't particularly recommend wading into Descartes, or indeed Athanasius. If I understand the argument correctly, there is a version of it in C. S. Lewis' *Miracles: A Preliminary Study* which is to my mind particularly cogent, although it is something of a variant of the original and will be considered later. The argument notes first that even if nothing else exists, I exist, that is, the person considering the question exists. (It is difficult to discuss, because at the ground level I do not know that you exist, and you do not know that I exist, so I cannot speak of what you know, only of what I know, which you then must take as what you know about your situation, whether or not I exist.) My existence is self-evident; but it is also limited. It is transient, that is, not continuous; I seem to cease to exist for periods when I am unconscious. More problematic, my existence has a definable beginning, a moment before which I have no memory of having existed, before which it seems quite certain that I did not exist. That, though, means that at some point my existence began, and therefore that there must be some cause of my being; there must in fact be some being that is not limited, not transient, not generated; a being with an eternal

---

[15] In Latin, *cogito ergo sum*.
[16] "Ontos" is the infinitive of the Greek verb "to be".

existence on which my own being is based or from which it is derived. Therefore something greater than I exists, something eternal, immortal, invisible, that has being in its own right, from which my being is drawn. That something is reasonably called "God".

I told you it was a difficult argument. All it proves about God (if indeed it proves anything) is that He exists, based on the recognition that something exists that has certain attributes we attribute to God. It does not really tell us that God is an eternally pre-existent being; it tells us that our existence is predicated on the existence of an eternally pre-existent being, and such a being would properly be called "God". Many who understand it find it unpersuasive; most who find it unpersuasive probably do not really understand it. I did not understand it the first several times I encountered it, but once it clicked I found it quite significant. Selfhood might be an illusion of mental process developed by evolution, but if so it is not a terribly significant thing and we can dismiss it as irrelevant. Yet it does not admit to being so easily dismissed, as if it were more than that, and it can only be significant if it is founded on something greater, a greater self.

Is that emotional? On one level, it is; it is a feeling that I have that says that I matter. Perhaps I do not matter; perhaps none of us matters. Yet I cannot escape the feeling that we do, and that is itself one of the data points to be considered: we can say that none of us matters, but we can never really feel as if that were true.[17]

---

[17] In the early 1970s, mathematician Kurt Godel published what is known as *Godel's Ontological Proof*, a complex

---

equation which he asserted proved the existence of God through a variant of this concept. The essence of it, translated into non-mathematical terms, is still a bit complicated. We can imagine God exists, taking God as that being for which no greater can be conceived. We also recognize that anything being real is greater than the exact same thing existing only as imaginary. The God we imagine is therefore greater if He exists than if He is merely imagined, so to be the greatest being we can conceive He must be real. This is, apparently, described mathematically. In 2013, two computer scientists in Berlin (named Christoph Benzmuller and Bruno Woltzenlogel Paleo) managed to solve the equation using a personal computer. They did so in order to demonstrate that computers are now able to solve our most complicated mathematical problems, but announced in the process that Godel was right. With Godel on the short list of the greatest logicians of all time (alongside Aristotle) it is difficult for any of even the most intelligent of us to assess quite what it is that the equation proves. However, he was smart enough to recognize the difference between proving that something real is greater than something imaginary and proving that it therefore must exist. It puts most of us in the awkward position, though, of having to take his word for it.

Cosmology

Existentialist philosopher Jean-Paul Sartre is cited as having said that the biggest problem with his philosophy was in the question, why is there something, rather than nothing? That is the foundation of the Cosmological Argument for the Existence of God,[18] that there is something, and that which exists cannot explain its own existence. We have pushed our scientific theories[19] to a beginning, presently to a singularity in which everything that would eventually become matter and energy was contained in a single dimensionless point which could not contain it all, and so it burst, creating space and forming into matter and energy as it moved outward—the Big Bang. We are not certain how everything managed to become constricted to such a point. Some suggest that it had happened before and will happen again, that although the universe is still expanding eventually the momentum of the initial push will be expended and the attraction of masses—gravity—will draw all matter, all energy, and even all space back into another singularity. Unfortunately, there is significant evidence to the effect that the universe will outrun the reach of gravity, and thus that all of this only happens once. The jury is still out. In one sense it does not matter; it is just easier to see the cosmological problem as long as the universe is

---

[18] "Kosmos" is the Greek noun for "world" or "universe".

[19] I call them theories without derogation; they are working hypotheses with ample evidence to support them, subject to adjustment in the future. I do not intend to imply by the term that they are in any sense not true, only that they are not known with absolute certainty and are still subject to revision as more data is collected.

thought to have a beginning—and part of the theory of the big bang suggests that time itself did not exist before the explosion.[20] Thus we have the problem that the universe seems to owe its origin to we know not what, and whatever that is, it has attributes we attribute to God.

Yet even if the universe is eternally pre-existent, it still triggers the cosmological argument. Sartre's problem is not that the universe could not have begun, but that it could not be, in the present. The most famous treatment of the cosmological argument comes from Thomas Aquinas, and it recognizes two different concepts of causality in this relationship. The familiar one is the easier one: if the universe had a beginning, something must have caused it to come into existence, and that something we take to be God. Yet the other is also true: if the universe has always existed, it does not appear to have qualities of independent existence. What causes it to be here? What causes anything to exist? Some will say we cannot answer that, we cannot know it; some will say it is not even a rational

---

[20] I have been particularly intrigued by Immanuel Kant's paradox about the beginning of the universe. If the universe is eternally pre-existent, without a beginning, then an infinite sequence of time must have passed to reach the present, and since an infinite sequence can never be completed, we cannot have reached the present. On the other hand, if time itself had a beginning, time being the medium in which change occurs, there can be no medium in which the change could have occurred from the universe not existing to the universe existing. It seems to me that as long as we are confined to the limits of the material universe, this paradox is fatal to the existence thereof, although I can see that there are possible understandings of the nature of time which might allow for either a beginning or an eternal pre-existence without triggering the paradox.

question, since obviously it is here and as far as we know it might always have been here. Yet its very rules—entropy, the big one—suggest that if it has always been here it ought to have ceased to exist, because it has had forever to disintegrate to nothing. Aquinas argued that the present and continued existence of the universe was a dependent existence, that even if it in fact had no beginning it still would be dependent on the existence of something greater than itself, a "first cause" which if not in time was still so in ontology, that the universe has dependent existence and could only have dependent existence if something else had independent existence, and thus that God exists.

If at this point you ask, "Who made God?" you have missed the point of the argument, or perhaps expected it to prove more than it does. What it asserts is that there must be a principle cause—whether first in time or first in causation—and that the universe in which we exist contains nothing that is not itself caused. The cause of the universe must be something outside the universe, and while we can imagine that that cause is itself caused, an infinite regression of causes could not exist, as there must be a principle cause which is the original cause of all other causes but is not itself caused. Certain (not all) conceptions of God fit that function, and at this point there is no suggestion of any other potential primary uncaused cause. Thus in simpler terms, the argument proves that something exists which causes the existence of the universe which is not itself caused by anything, and that our best guess for what that might be is what we call God.

We can accept Sartre's problem, and simply say that the universe exists and we cannot explain why, that the very ability to find the answer is beyond what is knowable. Yet there is a simple answer that potentially explains it, and no matter how we approach the issue, it seems that something must cause the universe to exist. It is again not conclusive, but it is rational evidence.

Teleology

In college I read perhaps three quarters of William Paley's famed *Evidences of the Christian Religion*, including the watch argument. (My reading was interrupted by a classmate who borrowed the book, took it home, and last saw it in his father's clutches.) I am also familiar with David Hume's response. Teleology[21] is also called The Argument From Design, and Paley's watchmaker example is still the clearest and most famous presentation of it.

The argument asserts that if you find a watch, you infer the existence of a watchmaker. Watches do not merely happen. Such machines are designed and constructed by intelligent persons with specific purposes. A similar illustration of the same principle is found in the notion of a dictionary being created by an explosion in a print shop. The principle here can be described, that irrational causes do not produce rational results, that working designs cannot happen by chance. The extrapolation, then, is that the universe runs as a working design, and thus an intelligence must have designed and built it, and any intelligence great enough to have done so would appropriately be called God.

Hume's response is based on probability. He agrees that it is entirely unlikely that a watch would simply come into existence at any particular point in time and space. However, he claims that it is not impossible for all the parts that would make a functional timepiece to fall together into a functional

---

[21] "Telos" is the Greek word for "end", including such meanings as goal and purpose.

timepiece—it is only unlikely in the extreme. He then asserts that the universe is comprised of infinite time and space, and given infinite time and space everything that might happen will happen, somewhere at some point in time. Thus even if the odds of the watch occurring accidentally are one in one decillion against, if you keep rolling the dice for an infinitely long time, eventually that number will appear, and you will have a functioning watch that happened by chance. In essence, this is the original form of the argument that if you give an infinite number of monkeys an infinite number of typewriters, one of them will produce a play by Shakespeare. It has more recently been suggested that the existence of the Internet has disproved this. It hasn't, really (what Internet posters write is not random), but it does suggest that Paley is right, that even well-designed literature requires intelligence to create.

Some respond to the argument with the counter-argument that the universe falls into the patterns it has because of the laws that govern it. When it is responded that those laws are the intelligent design that makes the universe possible, it leads to a disagreement concerning what constitutes design. It also leads to a more basic problem: if the universe did not work, that is, if the laws were not as they are, then we would not be having this conversation. Thus in any universe that failed to coalesce into some kind of order, there would be no such discussion and no one could argue that the lack of design demonstrates the non-existence of a designer. It is only because there is order that we infer design and thus a designer. Thus if the explosion caused the   dictionary,   the   monkeys   wrote   the

Shakespearean play, the watch happened by chance, then we are there to note that there is a dictionary, a play, a watch, and to conclude that someone created it; while if there is no dictionary, no play, no watch, there is also no discussion because there is no one to do the discussing.

It again returns to the issue of whether we have meaning. We exist; do we exist by accident, or by design? Even some of the top scientists today believe that there is a God who has designed it all. I lack their knowledge and cannot make an argument on that level. I do note that from my perspective, it seems awfully convenient that things are as they are. To some degree the argument can be made that it is we who are perfectly adapted to the way things are, and that were they different we would be perfectly adapted to however they were instead. Yet the complexity of relationships that make life as we know it possible, from the fact that the orbit of the moon stabilizes the axis of the earth creating relatively consistent climatic regions to the fact that water is the only substance which when it becomes a solid adjusts itself molecularly so as to be less dense than its liquid form, permitting ice to form and melt instead of collecting in the depths of the lakes and oceans, repeatedly raises points in which had this one thing been other than it is, there probably would not have been life on this planet.

Consider this. Imagine that on some future interstellar exploration there was found on a planet what appeared to be the remains of a great city, buildings in decay, utility lines, evidence of everything that would have been built by an intelligent race, but no signs of life. Will our explorers conclude that there must have been something like people who built it, or that by the most improbable of coincidences all of these materials and objects happened to fall into this shape, giving the impression of a city? Hume is asking us to believe that the latter is at least a plausible explanation of such a find; Paley is telling us that the appearance of a past civilization is convincing proof of a past civilization.[22]

The universe is that city, demonstrating the work of a creative mind. It makes little sense to suppose that it is a random occurrence.[23]

---

[22] Occam's Razor asserts that we should always embrace the simplest explanation for the evidence. The issue here is whether it is simpler to embrace a belief in a convergence of an unimaginably vast number of individually vastly improbable occurrences, or a belief that there was an intelligent designer behind what exists.

[23] Astrophysicist Neil DeGrasse Tyson has long argued that "intelligent design" is not a plausible scientific position and ought not be taught in schools. However, participating in the 2016 Isaac Asimov Memorial Debate at the American Museum of Natural History he asserted that the probability that the universe is just a simulation (very like the world depicted in *The Matrix*) "may be very high", and that he would not be surprised to discover that someone designed our universe in something like a computer. He did not note the inconsistency between this and his views on intelligent design. Paley's Watchmaker is more necessary if the universe is not real than if it is.

That does not begin to touch on the more difficult design issues, yet I find it quite compelling.[24]

---

[24] Some assert that the Apostle Paul referenced these first three arguments, and possibly the next ones, when he wrote in Romans 1:19f (quoting from the King James Version), "...that which may be known of God is manifest in them; for God hath shewed *it* unto them. [20] For the invisible things of him from the creation of the world are clearly seen, being understood by the things that are made, *even* his eternal power and Godhead...." Certainly Paul meant that the existence and design of the universe implies the existence of God, and these arguments reasonably expand on that foundation; to what degree Paul perceived the arguments as we know them is much less certain. However, it is apparent that even without these formulations of the arguments, the facts on which they are built strongly suggest the existence of a Creator. Most people, indeed most peoples, concluded that there was some kind of divine origin of the world. Evidence that compelling requires more than a casual response.

Moral

    I could not do this argument justice without stating that I first encountered it in *Mere Christianity*[25] by C. S. Lewis, and then again in his *Miracles: A Preliminary Study.*[26] I personally find this the most intriguing and compelling of the logical arguments I have encountered.

The observation is made that I, within myself, perceive that some things are in some sense "right", and others are "wrong". I have an innate feeling that I should do the "right" things, even when I don't want to, and I also feel that others ought to do the "right" things and not do the "wrong" things. It is evident that the "right" thing is not always advantageous, and the "wrong" thing often is. I have no particular desire to do "right"; rather, the urging to do "right" is frequently opposed to my desires, and sometimes tells me that I ought to encourage feeble desires and quash strong ones, such as the prompting to strengthen the weaker desire to defend the weak from oppressive bullies over the stronger desire to avoid harm to oneself.

    Wider observation reveals that most people speak and act as if they have this same sense, that some things are "right" and others "wrong". More significantly, these categories of "right" and "wrong" seem to align rather closely—that is, those things which I think are wrong are usually thought to be wrong by others.[27] This tendency toward

---

[25] ©1952 and subsequent, previously published in three books, *The Case for Christianity* ©1942, *Christian Behavior* ©1943, and *Beyond Personality* ©1944, various publishers.

[26] ©1947 and subsequent, various publishers.

[27] Some will no doubt object that there is disagreement on specific issues. The issue of abortion is a good example

uniformity in moral concepts is the more remarkable when you study world cultures and religions, and discover that all moral codes in history display agreement in most moral principles. We find a statement in ancient Egyptian writings that is echoed in the Eddas of the Vikings and again in the legends of the Native Americans and the writings of The Buddha, in every part of the world in all time.[28] We find it repeatedly. Somehow, humans everywhere agree on a remarkably unified conception of right and wrong. We try to teach our children to do right and avoid wrong, because for some reason even though we know what is right and what is wrong, we often want to do wrong and we often do wrong with full knowledge that it is wrong; yet even children raised without such parental guidance develop concepts of right and wrong that comport with the typical model. The feeling that he has been treated unfairly, or that one of his peers "cheated", or that someone ought not be allowed to do

---

because it is currently hotly contested. There is a tension here between the notion on the one hand that killing an unborn child is murder and on the other hand that forcing a woman to carry an unwanted child to term is a form of slavery. Those who favor abortion do not generally favor indiscriminate murder but rather believe that the circumstances place the woman's right to freedom from any form of enslavement above any right an unborn child might or might not have to life. Those who oppose abortion do not favor slavery generally but believe that the right to life of any innocent human attaches at conception and supercedes any claim that the mother might make to individual freedom. Both sides agree that murder is wrong and that slavery is wrong; they disagree as to whether in this particular instance the issue is murder or slavery.

[28] C. S. Lewis provides a fascinating collection of examples of such principles in an appendix in his *The Abolition of Man* (©1944 et cetera, various reprints from several publishers).

something which was done to him, are all reflections of this innate sense of justice. We create governments to punish those who do wrong, creating and enforcing rules we call laws.

In describing these concepts, we use words like "fair" and "just" and "equitable", and "righteous" versus "wicked", "good" versus "evil". We treat these concepts as if they were something real, having real force or meaning.

That is important. Right and wrong appear to be something other than our personal preferences; in fact, if they were our personal preferences, by their own standards it would be wrong for us to enforce them. That is, we punish those who steal, who destroy property, who injure and kill others, and we justify our punishment by asserting that they were wrong. Without that justification, our entire legal system devolves to people with one opinion ganging up against people with a different opinion. You cannot punish me for liking spinach nor I you for not liking it, because that is merely opinion, and even if most people agreed on one position we would not say that those of the opposing opinion were morally wrong and deserving of punishment, because it is merely an opinion. Yet we assert that our opinions about moral rectitude are not merely opinions, but recognitions of realities of some sort, that some things actually are wrong.

Some argue that these moral and ethical principles are part of an evolved survival mechanism, that we as a group have grown to embrace them because they are beneficial to the survival of the group. To this there are at least two objections. The first is that sometimes what is perceived to be the right thing for me to do does not benefit me at all, nor any of those with whom I am primarily concerned (my family and friends), as for example the claim that it is right for those who have abundance to share it with strangers who have nothing. That claim is meaningless if it is based on an evolutionary survival mechanism, because my own survival and the survival of my offspring are not at all enhanced and probably are threatened by the surrender of our abundance. Perhaps more pointedly, the claim that it is wrong for me and my family and friends to take by force what we need to ensure our own survival from others who will probably perish for lack of basic needs cannot be defended based on an evolutionary conception of survival. I might prefer it if that were not done to me, but if the point is to survive, the survival of my own people takes a natural evolutionary precedence over the survival of anyone else. It becomes right for me to kill them and take their goods, based on strictly pragmatic rules of morality. Yet we think this is wrong, and use words like "genocide" to decry such acts.

The second objection to this evolutionary claim is that the fact that particular principles are accepted because we have evolved in a fashion based on random responses to random influences yielding the most effective survival strategy cannot be the basis for an argument that those principles are "right", only that they have proved useful in the past; and many things which have proved useful in the past have been abandoned because they are not useful in the present and are not binding on us. The concept that men should go out and bring home food while women manage households and children has strong evolutionary roots impacting both the physical and psychosocial forms of our sexes, but is not generally considered to be a binding moral concept. Yet somehow these concepts are more than that. Some argue that such moral principles are varied and not accepted by all. There are certainly variations in concepts based on social circumstances and knowledge. The details of application of principles in equatorial Africa may differ from those in arctic Finland. Yet there is nonetheless remarkable similarity across all cultures. There have also been people who deny being held to any universal moral code, and yet it is evident that they have their own moral code and are conversant in the same concepts of morality, equity, and justice as everyone else. They either deny that everyone else is protected by that morality (it applies only within the tribe) or they pretend that the code does not exist as a foil to reject criticism from others (we are not obligated to your concept of morality). Very few people lack this concept of fairness, random individuals we label "sociopaths", and it is questionable whether they actually do not have the sense of fairness or simply choose to ignore it.[29]

The objection persists that even within our own culture there is disagreement on individual issues.

---

[29] Francis Schaeffer gives the example (in *Death in the City*, ©1969, Intervarsity Press) of the Marquis de Sade, who wrote an extensive moral philosophy which asserted that whatever is is right, and on that basis justified his own cruelty toward women, that because men are physically stronger than women they have the inherent right to dominate them. In the end of his life when he was in prison, his philosophy apparently abandoned him, as he wrote that the guards were treating him unfairly. He could clearly recognize the accepted concepts of injustice when he was at the receiving end.

Yet the disagreements themselves are informative, because they prove to be disagreements in application of fundamental principles. Each side argues that its position is "right" and the other "wrong" by appealing to a deeper concept of what is right and what is wrong, and attempting to extend the agreed concepts to the present applications. A nineteenth century rancher who stole water from another rancher's land would be recognized as a thief. Such a rancher upstream from another rancher who dammed the streams to keep the water on his property would argue that his right of possession makes this the right thing for him to do to provide for his cattle (and indirectly for his family), while the downstream neighbor would argue that this is theft of the water that should flow onto his land— water which he has never had in his possession, but expected would reach him by the normal course of events. At that point, the question is not whether stealing water is wrong, but whether the upstream rancher is in fact stealing water by preventing it from escaping his property. In similar ways moral arguments are usually not about the basic moral principles but about the application of those principles and precedence of one over another in specific situations. Both parties assume that the other agrees with the basic principles upon which the arguments are based. Without that fundamental agreement, there could be no meaningful argument.

Thus the problem is that this attitude virtually all humans share about good and evil, wrong and right, justice and injustice, cannot be explained adequately by any natural explanation and still retain any validity. As soon as we explain, naturalistically, why everyone has these feelings about right and wrong, we invalidate any legitimacy that they might have had and reduce our justice system to the strong (whether it is the strength of the superior fighters of feudalism or of the superior numbers of democracy) imposing their will upon the weak.

For concepts of equity or justice or fairness to have any *moral* force, any basis beyond that those who have power choose to enforce them against those without power, they must be something other than a natural development or pragmatically convenient set of rules. Since they are not really ever what we desire to do, and are not always what is most advantageous for us individually, they have all the marks of someone trying to tell us how we ought to live.

There is a circular nature to the argument against morality at this point, precisely because it is a moral argument about morality. The core concept is that it is unfair for people to do to others what they would not want done to themselves, and thus we attempt to enforce that on others which we would not want enforced on ourselves. Yet if morality[30] is a pragmatic convenience which naturally developed, then the enforcement of morality is one of those pragmatic conveniences. In this conception, we do not enforce laws against stealing or murder because

---

[30] Although it should be obvious, this is not speaking of the narrow concept of *sexual* morality, but the broader concept of morality as that which is just or equitable. All once-good words for this in English have been subverted to other concepts, such that "morality" now refers to sexual issues, "ethics" to professional standards, "righteousness" and "holiness" to religious piety, and "justice" to judicial and legislative decisions. Here we are speaking of the concepts of rightness and wrongness themselves, not any specific application of them.

these things are wrong and it is right to prevent them, but because we have a preference for a society in which they are forbidden and a preference to use such force as we are able to bring to bear to forbid them. The deeper problem not seen here is that if this is so, then whatever group is in power can enforce whatever rules it prefers for its own advantage. No overriding principle, such as the equitable distribution of resources or the good of the many, can override this practical concept if all justice or morality ultimately means is that which those in power find convenient for the benefit of society as they want it. Ultimately, though, either morality has some basis beyond the natural order to which we can appeal in claiming that something is right or just and something else is wrong or unfair, or all such appeals amount to a statement that the person making such a claim would prefer that some actions be encouraged and others discouraged for entirely practical and personal reasons.

We might look at this problem from a different direction. People who feel they have been wronged frequently make the statement that the person who wronged them "had no right". Let us suppose a simple invasion of privacy, that one person has a private notebook, diary, or journal, and another reads from it without permission. The person who wrote these secrets declares that the other had no right to invade his private thoughts. That inherently asserts that the person who wrote those thoughts has a right to keep such thoughts, and such writings, private, and that the other person has no higher right to invade them.

It might be argued that such rights are a modern invention. Certainly a millennium ago no one would have written anything he did not want anyone else to read, because such a concept of a "right to privacy" had not been articulated. Yet that puts us in a quandary. If we say that such a right did not then exist, we make it a modern invention and its validity amounts to that we choose, corporately, to believe that there is such a right. That means that we have a consensus of opinion on the matter; it does not mean that such a right really exists in any way beyond that we recognize and enforce it—in essence that we bully those who impinge on such a right by taking other rights away from them. It becomes a matter of opinion, in which the opinion of the many is enforced against the opinion of the few, a violation of the very right that the many wish to uphold.

Thus we must rather say that such a right did exist a thousand years ago, and simply was not recognized. Yet if that is the case, if the right has existence independent of being recognized, then morality must exist in a supernatural way, that is, in a way that causes it to be imposed on us and our human realm by something greater than it and outside it.

Thus in order for words like "fair" and "just" and "equitable" and "right" to have a genuine meaning distinct from "useful", "practical", and "preferred", there has to be something or someone which or who has in some way communicated these concepts to us. That someone is reasonably identified as God; and the moral argument tells us that this God is intelligent and fair, that He fits our understanding of that which is good.[31]

---

[31] Putting it in terms familiar to most Americans, Thomas Jefferson was able to speak of "inalienable rights" because (as

---

a Deist) he could say that humans were "endowed by their creator".   If there is no creator, there are no "inalienable rights", only contractual ones, those we have by consensus and agreement.   If the terms of the agreement change, so do our supposed rights.   Any talk of "human rights" can be nothing less than a claim that there is a divine right for humans to be treated in a specified fashion; without that, such talk means no more than "I don't like what you're doing."

Intellect

In his book *Miracles: A Preliminary Study*,[32] C. S. Lewis restates aspects of the Moral Argument which he had expounded in *Mere Christianity*,[33] but first presents a similar but distinct argument based on the intellect. I have more recently wondered whether this is a variant of the ontological argument, but if so it is a much simpler one to grasp and one that is distinct in several ways.

To begin, we need to step away from the details and recognize that on the broadest possible level we are distinguishing a naturalist view of the universe from a supernaturalist view. The naturalist view holds that the universe is complete and cohesive within itself, that everything that happens is entirely explained within the system. Whatever other realms might exist, they are irrelevant to this one. The agnostic who asserts that there is no evidence for the existence of God and thus no reason to believe that one exists is arguing for naturalism.

The opposing view is supernaturalism, which obviously believes that there is something beyond or above nature, something outside the material universe, and that that supernatural realm is relevant. It would be the nature of the supernatural realm, inherent in the concept, that it could interfere with the natural realm without being subject to it; that is, it is outside the world in the sense that the players are outside the game, except that the world might be able to continue without supernatural interference

---

[32] Op. Cit.

[33] Op. Cit. Technically which were in *The Case for Christianity*, the first of the three books composed of his radio lectures which were combined ultimately into one volume.

(whereas a game ceases when all players stop playing). One could not perform an experiment to prove the existence of the supernatural realm, because causes in the natural world would not necessarily have effects in the supernatural, even though the supernatural world could interfere with the natural.

As we are thinking about this, it must not escape our notice that we are, in fact, *thinking* about it. When we discuss it, we present observations and arguments and conclusions, all of which are aspects of a rational process. We gather facts and form arguments, and accept that the conclusions we reach are valid, that is, either true or likely to be true. Yet we ignore our epistemology: on what basis do we believe that these thought processes are themselves rational, as opposed to being random physiological events akin to heart palpitations, or responses to stimuli akin to sneezes? What justification do we have to assert that anything we conclude by use of our reason is what we call "true"?

One answer, of course, is "none at all". Increasingly modern intellectuals are adopting this answer, that mental process is itself suspect, and that all the rules we have devised concerning what constitutes a valid logical argument or a logical fallacy are so much sophistry. We do not really know anything, and certainly cannot rely on our rational abilities to reach the level of certainty we call truth. This is the unavoidable conclusion of a thoroughly naturalist position: random chains of events, themselves irrational, following random rules, themselves established by irrational chains of events, have created an organ within the human body which responds to stimuli in such a way that its random electrical discharges and chemical formations cause us to have consciousness and a mode of what we call thought which has practical use in living our lives but which is not in any sense valid or reliable. It can record environmental information, such as that meat that smells like something dead will make you sick if you eat it, and if you strike two hard rocks together you can create sparks which will cause fires. It cannot tell us that the smell of something dead comes from toxins excreted by microorganisms digesting the meat, or that fire is a chemical reaction in which elements such as carbon or hydrogen are combining with oxygen at an accelerated rate releasing energy as they do so. Those explanations are themselves not actually observations but conclusions from observations. The chain, "When I have consumed this chemical, I have gotten sick, therefore the chemical makes me sick," is a logical conclusion, inherently suspect because it relies on our presumed rational processes to reach.[34]

Therein lies the problem. People can say that rational processes are unreliable random events which produce useful results but cannot be presumed to reach truth, but we all act otherwise. We treat thought, and particularly structured logical argument, as if it were reliable, both in our intellectual pursuits and in our daily lives. We allow that reasoning from evidence gives us valid conclusions in our science; we reject statements that

---

[34] It may help to grasp this if we suggest alternatives, such as "This substance is holy to the gods, and if I consume it the gods will strike me with illness." Objectors will say that that is an irrational statement, but the fundamental question is whether an evaluation of a statement as "rational" itself has any meaning.

are based on logical fallacies entirely because of those fallacies. Naturalism gives us no basis for doing so, and the principles of logic which we have developed, notably that irrational causes do not reliably produce rational results, lead inexorably to the conclusion that our principles of logic are unreliable. Any proof that naturalism is true is in essence a proof that all proofs are invalid including itself.

To argue logically at all, we must assume that such mental processes are valid. They can be so if they are not caused by random natural events, but come into the natural order from outside or beyond it. This assumes that there is a supernatural realm, and that something in that realm is capable of producing rational thought independent of random causes. That is, our very ability to think is either something given from a supernatural realm by something like a god, or it is a completely irrational string of arrant nonsense which we mistakenly take for rational logic because we are unable to know otherwise.

I note that this does not in any sense prove the existence of God. What it demonstrates is that the non-existence of God would make proof impossible, because we could never reach the point at which logic were itself validated, and every supposed logical statement we ever made would be suspect, potentially fallacious, by the very standard we imagine exists but which actually cannot and does not exist. If God does not exist, we can stop talking about it, and about everything else, because not only can we not know anything, we cannot know that we cannot know.

The existence of God thus becomes a necessary presupposition to all discourse, because if there is not something like God giving us rational thought, we cannot have the kind of rational thought we think we have.

The Good Man

To me, though, the most compelling argument
for the existence of God is an historical argument,
that is, an argument based on events in history. I
conclude from the evidence that God revealed
Himself, making a one-time appearance in the midst
of human history in the person of Jesus. Having
taken this human life, He delivered a teaching which
was simultaneously strictly moral and openly loving
and merciful. He directly and indirectly claimed to
be God, and more tellingly spoke and acted in ways
fully consistent with that claim.   Further, He
performed feats that clearly bent the natural order
yet were fundamentally consistent with it, feats
which we call miracles and which the Bible often
calls signs, because they demonstrated Who He was.
When all the evidence is given a fair hearing, it
admits only one conclusion, that this man actually
was Who He claimed to be, the human embodiment
of God in the world.

Of course, if you reach that conclusion, you are
forced to accept that there is a God, that He is
involved in what happens in this world, and that the
Christian message is if not the truth then the closest
approximation to the truth we have. Since many
people would rather the Christian message not be
true, for many different reasons, efforts are made to
invalidate the evidence. We are told by some that
there is no evidence Jesus actually ever lived, by
others that he lived but we have no reliable accounts
of his life. In order for the historic evidence that
God lived among men to be considered, it has to be
accepted as valid. You do not have to believe that
the Bible is the infallible or inerrant Word of God to

consider the evidence; you need only treat it as you would any other historical source, giving it only as much credibility as it earns from its own credentials. As it turns out, those credentials are remarkably strong, such that events recorded in the New Testament are more reliably reported than most of the events of ancient history which we accept.

I do not expect you to take my word for this; on the other hand, it would be silly of me to rehash the volumes of evidence which others have capably presented. I have read works by textual critic Bruce M. Metzger (whom I have met) and by biblical historian F. F. Bruce; their valuable knowledge in their fields and that of other scholars is covered generally in the books of Lee Strobel as well as in detail in their own books. Rather, I will touch on a few of the most cogent points and let the reader pursue the data in more detail in those sources if he wants more information. We will approach it by looking at the objections.

The starting point for our objectors seems to have been that miracles do not happen, and since miracles do not happen we must find an explanation for why they are reported to have happened in these accounts of the life of Jesus. The accounts themselves must be unreliable, since they report events that are impossible.

It should be noted that this starting point is both disingenuous and circular. The entire point of the miracle accounts is that the writers believed things were happening which they thought were impossible and therefore miraculous. It will not do to argue that the writers or the people believed these things were happening because lacking any scientific education they did not understand them to be impossible. Had they not recognized that these were disruptions in the natural order, they would have had no interest in them. It is because they were impossible that they were reported at all. Thus we cannot dismiss the accounts as stories of simple people who did not recognize that these were violations of the laws of science, because absent some understanding of what we call the laws of science (and they would have called the normal course of life), there would be no such accounts.

More on point, at issue is whether these things occurred, and if the first assumption is that they did not, then we are fitting the evidence to our conclusion rather than drawing the conclusion from the evidence. That is, the argument seems to be, "Since there are no reliable accounts of miracles, miracles must be impossible, and therefore any accounts of miracles are unreliable." Yet if we dismiss the evidence perfunctorily, we cannot arrive at an honest opinion on the subject, because we have evaluated the evidence not on its merits but on our opinion. We might think that miracles are unlikely in the extreme, but if we begin by asserting they are impossible then we have prejudiced the case unjustifiably. We cannot know that miracles are impossible; we must examine the evidence in favor of them and the evidence against them and reach a conclusion based on the evidence.

This also applies to the claims Jesus made of divinity. Many would like to say that He was a simple but great moral teacher, and that His followers invented the notion that He was God and then back wrote the stories to include that. We need to evaluate the evidence itself on its own merits, not

45

on our opinion concerning what we want the answer to be.

Origins of the Documents

The first explanation that was given was simple: the accounts we have, the four "Gospels" and the Book of Acts of the Apostles, are not the contemporary accounts by the eyewitnesses that they claim to be, but compilations of tales gathered over several centuries and composed much later by anonymous Christians who then attached the names of prominent persons to these.   Never mind that Luke and Mark are only prominent because they wrote the books attributed to them (they are mentioned rather sparingly otherwise), the church needed writings that told the stories which had been passed by word of mouth, and they created these to fill that purpose.

In the absence of any evidence, such a theory seems to have merit on its face.   We know, for example, that the writings related to Mohammed are easily identified as some which are contemporary with the events and contain his teachings, and some which were written several centuries later attributing miracles to him.   Assuming that the accounts of the miracles are untrue and the claims of divinity are a later invention, these can all be explained in the oral tradition process of passing information from generation to generation by word of mouth.   It explains away everything.   It was fully expected that over time we would discover that the historic and cultural references were inaccurate, inventions of a later age.   The problem is, it was never the case that there was no evidence, and as more evidence has been gathered the idea has completely collapsed.

Simply examining the books, we find them riddled with the marks of eyewitness accounts—the young man who escapes the scene of the arrest by slipping out of his clothes when grabbed,[35] Jesus poking in the dirt when they brought him the woman caught in adultery,[36] the fact that the Galilean tax collector Matthew reported facts concerning Jesus' birth that would have been recalled by his Galilean businessman father[37] while the careful historian Luke who conducted extensive interviews to form his account had the details only His mother Mary, reported by him to have been in Jerusalem in the early days of the church,[38] would have known.[39] One could only have reached the conclusion that these were not the eyewitness accounts they

---

[35] Mark 14:51f.

[36] John 8:2ff. This passage is challenged by many because of issues with its location in the text, but it contains several marks of authenticity of which the report of Him poking in the dirt is only one. It may be as C. S. Lewis suggests that very early the account was removed from many copies of the book to discourage interpreting it as approving adultery, or as I have speculated that it was one of the "Q" fragments that did not find a place in any of the Gospels but was preserved separately and then incorporated later. The very fact that we have this kind of textual evidence concerning this one passage supports the contention that the rest of the documents were composed early and preserved in their original form.

[37] Matthew 1:1-1:21; it is generally thought that the genealogy reported by Matthew is that of Joseph.

[38] Acts 1:14.

[39] Luke 1:5-2:51. Of particular note is that Luke more than once comments that Mary "treasured all these things in her heart," committing them to memory, which strongly suggests that he got the accounts from her. It also tells us that John the Baptist's mother was related to Mary, giving a connection for the information about the birth of John. The genealogy reported by Luke in Luke 3:23ff is generally thought to be that of Mary.

purported to be by beginning with that conclusion
and ignoring the evidence in the text.

Even so, this once-popular notion had to be
rejected based on other evidence. We have extant
writings of authors from the second century, at the
beginning of which Clement of Rome makes clear
reference to there being four Gospel accounts and by
the middle of which they are identified as having
been written by Matthew, Mark, Luke, and John.
By the end of that century they were treated as
authoritative, equal to the Old Testament scriptures
in value, and it is impossible to imagine that those
original accounts were lost and replaced by others,
or that they were significantly altered. That, though,
is another objection to which we will return in a
moment. These second century authors also quoted
from those books in their writings, and while it was
only a sentence here and a sentence there it was
always sufficient to identify the books from which
they were quoting.[40]   It is quite remarkable that
presumably educated scholars once somehow
believed that second century writers quoted from
books that were not written until the third or fourth
century.

As we have continued to study ancient copies of
scripture, we have identified copies—complete
copies of multiple books, such as all the Pauline
letters or all the non-Pauline letters or all the gospels
—dating back well into the early second century.
We also have found fragments—bits of paper with a

---

[40] I am informed that among the extant writings of the Church
Fathers through the seventh century the entire New Testament
appears in snippets and quotations but for three verses; these
quotations are often used by textual critics as cross-
confirmation of the text. I do not know how much is extant
from second century writings.

few dozen words on them—from the latter half of the first century. They were clearly already in circulation before the end of the first century, having gained acceptance by people alive during the events they recounted. It cannot be maintained with any credibility that the books were composed later.[41]

---

[41] Fragments of what is clearly a copy of the Gospel according to Matthew in book form, popularly known as the "Jesus Papyrus", are plausibly dated to not later than 50 A.D., strongly suggesting that copies of this book were already in circulation before that, less than two decades after the crucifixion.

Preservation of the Texts

Once that argument fell, the next raised was that indeed such books existed, but they have changed so much since then that we do not have them in their original forms. This argument takes two forms, the one that this happened accidentally simply because the books had to be hand-copied and errors crept in, the other that there was a conspiracy among church leaders to create a Bible that taught what they wanted taught.   Both of these notions badly misrepresent conditions in the early centuries of the church and the facts concerning the transmission of these documents.

Those second century authors previously mentioned did communicate with each other, but they were not near neighbors. They lived in such disparate locations as Rome in Italy, Alexandria in Egypt, Antioch in Syria, Smyrna in Turkey, and Carthage in North Africa.[42] They each had their own copies of these books, which they preserved separately, and from which they in essence argued as they attempted to understand the "doctrine" within them. To have agreed to alter these not only would have been contrary to their attitudes toward the text, it would have been a logistical nightmare. There was no central clearinghouse of approved text, and the copies that exist today can be traced through the equivalent of familial lines to sources.

---

[42] It is also significant that these cities are relatively evenly connected to the Roman Catholic, Eastern Orthodox, and Coptic Churches, early divisions based on doctrinal and polity disagreements. These divisions speak volumes against claims of collusion, as the theological disagreements can be traced back through the writings from each area; yet the texts from which they argued were agreed.

The claim that the church conspiratorially altered the documents won't stand; efforts by early heretics to make such changes were quashed from all sides not because there was a dictated standard text but because there were multiple sources scattered throughout the world that were in agreement.

Of course, over the centuries errors did appear in the various texts; but the texts were preserved in many places, and it was unlikely in the extreme that the same mistake made in North Africa would also be made in Syria or Rome. Thus our textual critics[43] pour over hundreds of copies, tracing where an error originated and what the original text said. Early translations, such as the King James Version, suffered from the absence of such research, but modern translations work from a text that is very nearly one hundred percent certified as the original. It is thus extremely clear that the text we have is a remarkably good record of the original, better than any other documents from the same age.[44] It is also incidentally clear that the text was extremely well preserved, as the discrepancies have been minimal,

---

[43] Bruce M. Metzger has already been named; others, working backwards roughly from the present into the eighteenth century, include Barbara Aland, Johannes Karavidopoulos, Carlo Martini, Zane C. Hodges, Allen Wikgren, Arthur L. Farstad, Kurt Aland, Matthew Black, Erwin Nestle, José Maria Bover, Alexander Souter, Augustinus Merk, Freiherr von Soden Hermann, Eberhard Nestle, Richard Francis Weymouth, Brooke Foss Westcott, Fenton John Anthony Hort, Constantin von Tischendorf, and Karl Lachmann.

[44] Questions concerning the text of the Old Testament are distinct and have their own problems and their own answers. Since we are dealing with whether the records of the life and words of Jesus are accurate, and since my expertise is focused on the New Testament, this is limited to those issues.

usually easily explained and corrected, and mostly unimportant to the meaning of the text.

We thus face documents that have more credibility as historic eyewitness accounts than any others in history. The events presented in the Gospels are better attested than any prior to perhaps the American Revolution. It is barely worth mentioning that there are incidental references to Jesus and his followers in such contemporary secular historians as Josephus and Philo and Tacitus, or that none of the predicted errors in the original composition have ever emerged. For example, despite the complexity of the Roman political system, Luke always gets titles and forms of address correct for the time and place, whether prefects or governors or tetrarchs or some other identification. Historic events such as appointments of officials to office when they have been confirmed always fit the accounts. These authors knew their milieu because it was theirs; they gave us the facts as accurately as anyone could.

Substance of the Evidence

We thus are faced with the unavoidable conclusion that the Gospel accounts present us with the genuine person of Jesus, what He said and what He did, and that the miracles and the claims of divinity are genuine events, whatever we make of them otherwise. We might explain a particular healing as entirely psychosomatic, but we cannot dismiss it as not a true account and must address the details.

To my mind, the miracles are actually the lesser problem. If indeed Jesus was Who and what the accounts say He claimed to be, that He performed miracles seems almost incidental. The one exception is also the best attested, that He returned to life after having died. To this, we have a clear indication that He was dead, killed in a very effective manner, certified as dead by Roman soldiers who were very good at killing people.[45] His body was given not to His inner circle, but to two Jewish leaders who while they thought He might be a prophet and questioned Him during His life were hardly in a position to be co-conspirators in any kind of plot, who interred him in a tomb with a seal and a

---

[45] The spear that pierced His side is a significant point in this. It is reported in John 19:34 that when his side was pierced there was an immediate release of blood and water together. This is followed by the author's assertion that this is an eyewitness account of the event, but no explanation of why there would be both blood and water. Modern physiology has concluded that this would be the result of a burst heart and the accompanying collapse of the lymphatic fluid into the bloodstream—clear proof that Jesus was dead, but not a detail anyone at the time would have invented, not having the understanding of physiology to suggest it.

Roman guard. It appears that He vanished from the tomb, leaving the burial wrappings behind; once the stone was moved (apparently by a supernatural messenger sent for that purpose) it was observed that the tomb was already empty. The empty tomb was never a point of argument in those first years of the church, in some part because the Jewish leaders immediately did damage control, reporting that the disciples stole the body (amazing that they overcame the armed and trained Roman guards[46]), but in greater part because they had seen Him. We have some of the accounts of His appearances after His death, and the indication that there were quite a few more. He appeared sometimes to individuals, to small groups, once to five hundred people gathered together.[47] Their argument was never that the tomb

---

[46] Some are confused by the point that when the Sanhedrin requested that Pilate post a guard on the tomb the governor told them to post their own guards, and thus that in one account these are Temple guards. It is a moot point: the Sanhedrin was an officially recognized governing body in Jerusalem, and thus the guards to which Pilate refers are Roman guards assigned to Sanhedrin authority. Note that when Jesus was arrested it was by Roman guards who took Him to the Sanhedrin, not to the governor, because they were a detail assigned to the Sanhedrin.

[47] Some argue that the appearances were hallucinatory. The very variety of times, places, and conditions reported for those appearances suggests that a conscious effort was made to demonstrate that they were not—sometimes in closed rooms, sometimes on lakeshores or walking on roads, sometimes to individuals and sometimes to crowds. Always conversations occurred, and frequently several persons were involved and thus obviously hearing the same words from the supposed hallucinatory participant. We have no other credible account of shared hallucinations of this sort; those who hold to that theory are grasping at straws because they consider the resurrection to be so completely impossible that no other

was empty; it was that they had seen Him alive and well after He had been crucified and interred, and that He was very much physically alive and present among them while at the same time different, more powerful, perhaps more alive, than anyone had ever been before. Anyone who comes to the records must deal with that as a reported eyewitness account from multiple eyewitnesses. It cannot be dismissed as a later accretion because it was the message from the beginning.[48] It cannot be dismissed as a mistake or hallucination because it was shared by independent witnesses. It cannot be dismissed as a conspiracy because all of the supposed conspirators were painfully executed without a single one recanting—difficult to imagine them doing that even given that it is true, but that they agreed to promote a lie and all held to it into a painful execution is unimaginable.

So the miracles, even the resurrection itself, are merely likely events given the truth of the claim to divinity. Arguably, one could reach the conclusion that Jesus was God based solely on the miracles He performed; but the accounts give us much more, including his own testimony on the subject.

There is little point to recounting all the times when Jesus made statements equating Himself with God, such as "I and the Father are one,"[49] or "Before

---

impossibility is as great. Yet if His claims of divinity are true, His resurrection seems very nearly necessary.

[48] Even those who reject early dates for the historic books of the New Testament acknowledge that at least most of Paul's letters to churches are mid first century documents, and the resurrection appears consistently in these as the foundation of the message.

[49] John 10:30.

Abraham was, I Am."[50] Nor is it necessary to recount all those incidents in which someone else stated it and He agreed, such as when Peter confessed this[51] or when the High Priest made it an accusation.[52] To say that He believed He was God seems fairly straightforward; you could avoid it only by deciding that the accounts were flawed. Yet even this does not resolve the matter, because it is not merely that He made those claims, but that He acted as if they were true in ways most of us would miss. He claimed that He could change the rules concerning the Sabbath;[53] He asserted that the miracles He did pointed to Who He was.[54] A study of those miracles strongly suggests that He had a natural poetic sense of how God did things—He made bread out of wheat (already baked as bread), fish out of fish (already caught and killed), but did not make bread from stones; He made wine from water, as grapes have done for centuries; He walked on water as many insects and some larger animals do. His miracles were always consistent with the natural order even while being very much beyond it.[55]

---

[50] John 8:58.

[51] Matthew 16:16.

[52] Matthew 26:63ff, Mark 14:61ff, Luke 22:66ff.

[53] Matthew 12:8, Mark 2:28, Luke 6:5. The keeping of the Sabbath itself was one of the Ten Commandments, and although how that was done was established through centuries of interpretive tradition, it would have appeared blasphemous for any one person to suggest that the Law itself did not mean what had been made of it.

[54] John 10:25ff.

[55] *Miracles: A Preliminary Study*, by C. S. Lewis, op. cit.

He healed bodies, much as healing occurs naturally, but often He connected the healing of the body with forgiveness of sins, which He claimed was also something He could legitimately do.[56] This escapes our notice, because we are accustomed to the notion of priests and ministers telling us our sins are forgiven as if they were doing it; but they are not doing it, they are telling us that God has done it. Jesus claimed to have the authority to forgive sins.[57] Again, it escapes our notice because we do not really understand what that means. It means that if I had an affair with your spouse, Jesus might come to me and tell me it is all right, that He forgives me for what I did to you. That is either the height of arrogance, or the recognition that He, and not you, is the person primarily wronged by my crime. In every way and at every turn, He acted as if He were God, but at the same time that He was defining for us what God is really like, one who teaches, who serves, who loves and cares for us and wants us to come to Him.[58]

It is thus inescapably apparent that Jesus consistently projected the claim that He is God. He was either right or wrong; if He was wrong He either lied or was deluded. Yet it is difficult to

---

[56] E.g., Matthew 9:2ff, Mark 2:5ff, Luke 5:20ff, Luke 7:47ff.

[57] Matthew 9:6, Mark 2:10, Luke 5:24. This point was not lost on His original audience—in two of those accounts, in Mark 2:7 and Luke 5:21, the Jewish leaders had just made the objection that only God can forgive sins; they certainly knew that the sacrifices made by the priests obtained forgiveness for the worshippers, but saw the distinction between giving assurance of forgiveness and giving forgiveness itself.

[58] Interestingly, most people who believe in what they take to be a non-specific version of God embrace the model Jesus presented.

examine the accounts of His life and reach either of those conclusions. He seems so honest and so sane.

Certainly some people have decided that He was a charlatan, but they cannot explain why if it was all an act He let it go so far as His execution—Pilate would have released Him if He had merely recanted, and the Sanhedrin would have let Him go if they could have had His disavowal. Others have decided He was crazy, but then cannot explain how He managed to motivate so many people from so many walks of life, religious leaders, professionals, businessmen, women, street people, revolutionaries, and more hanging on his words. Nor can they account for the rationally consistent melding of justice and mercy, law and love, that permeates His teaching.

It also does not explain that problem of the resurrection. No matter how you approach it, there is only the one explanation. The disciples did not steal the body or they could not have died for the lie. The Sanhedrin did not steal the body or they would have produced it to prove He had not been resurrected. The Romans did not steal the body or they would have produced it to exonerate their soldiers. The body simply left the tomb, and then He was seen, and physically touched, and seen eating and drinking, very much alive, by hundreds of witnesses.[59]

---

[59] It is foolishness to argue that all of the witnesses were believers. We know specifically that James and Paul were not believers until after Jesus appeared to them, and it is hard to imagine that anyone who saw Him alive after His death and knew what they were seeing would not become a believer.

In the end, it seems to me unavoidable that if we allow any historic validity to the accounts at all, Jesus was and is God; and if Jesus is God, not only does God exist, the Christian message, rightly understood, is true.

Concerning Eyewitness Accounts

Some object that eyewitness testimony is unreliable as evidence; that the fact that this is all based on what people claim to have seen and heard in itself makes it suspect. That has become very popular in legal theory and psychology in recent decades, and needs to be addressed.

First, although arguably eyewitness testimony is suspect, it is the best evidence we have for any events in history. Our knowledge of the Holocaust, of the American Civil War, of the Protestant Reformation and the Spanish Inquisition, are all primarily based on eyewitness accounts, whether recorded by the witnesses themselves or gathered by historians. We also have archaeological evidence, but as anyone who has read *Digging the Weans*[60] knows, the interpretation of archaeological evidence is highly questionable absent some historic records to which to connect it.

Second, all evidence is open to doubt and interpretation. Experimental evidence relies on the integrity of the experiment and the observations and sometimes assumptions of the experimenter. Forensic evidence similarly ultimately is the educated opinion of the examiner. In our courts, all real evidence is testimony—whether the testimony of someone who saw the events or the testimony of someone who examined artifacts of the scene and drew conclusions from them. (The fingerprint itself

---

[60] An article by Robert Nathan originally published in Harper's Magazine, later expanded to a book, in which the author humorously interprets the archaeological evidence unearthed from a place called "Pound Laundry", an apparently important city of a nation that referred to itself simply by the pronoun "WE", or in the accusative case, "US".

is not evidence in court; it is the testimony of the fingerprint expert to the effect that this fingerprint places the accused at the crime scene that is evidence in court.) Whether eyewitness testimony is better or worse than other evidence is certainly a debated topic in the present, but it is often the best kind of evidence we can have for certain information.

Third, in evaluating evidence, we must take into account the reliability of that evidence specifically. The New Testament offers quite a few points supporting its reliability.

On the matter of the resurrection of Jesus, we have written testimony from eight separate authors (Matthew, Mark, Luke, John, Paul, and Peter specifically mention the resurrection; the unidentified author of Hebrews speaks of Jesus' death and bodily ascension, and James of His anticipated return which implies His ascension); their written testimony often includes reference to the oral testimony of many others, over five hundred persons who claimed to have seen Jesus alive after his death. Further, as mentioned, it was not a single appearance but multiple appearances—at least eleven that we can distinguish, and the suggestion that there were quite a few others not individually recorded.[61] We are not relying on a single

---

[61] In as near an order as can be composed, we have reports of appearances to Mary Magdalene at the tomb (John 20:14ff), the other women on their way back from the tomb (Matthew 28:9, possibly the same appearance), Peter alone before the others (Luke 24:34, I Corinthians 15:5ff), two disciples one of whom was named Clopas on the road to Emmaus (Luke 24:13ff, Mark 16:12), the disciples together later on the day of the resurrection (Luke 24:36ff, John 20:19ff, I Corinthians 15:5ff) apparently without Thomas, a gathering of five hundred

questionable sighting by one person, but on many sightings including conversations involving multiple people, sharing meals, and hearing Him teach in the manner that was familiar to them.

As to the reported miracles, it is not one account of one miracle that is in question but multiple accounts of multiple miracles. The feeding of the multitudes is significant in this regard. We have the report that on one occasion He fed five thousand (Matthew 14:13ff, Mark 6:35ff, Luke 9:12ff, John 6:1ff), apparently in the wilderness near Bethsaida; it is reported by all four of the Gospels. At another time, in another place, he also fed four thousand persons (Matthew 15:29ff, Mark 8:1ff), apparently having occurred by a mountain near the Sea of Galilee. These are not, as some would suggest, contradictory accounts of the same event; both Matthew and Mark report both miracles, and both also report a conversation in which Jesus speaks of both miracles as separate events (Matthew 16:8ff, Mark 8:17ff). Similarly, dozens of healings and

---

(I Corinthians 15:5ff), James, presumably the one identified as the "brother of the Lord" (I Corinthians 15:5ff), the disciples including Thomas eight days after the resurrection (John 20:26ff, probably I Corinthians 15:5ff), the disciples in a surprise meeting by the Sea of Galilee (called Tiberius in this passage, John 21:1ff), the disciples in an assigned rendezvous on a mountain in Galilee (Matthew 28:16ff), the disciples in or near Jerusalem forty days after the resurrection on the day of the ascension (Acts 1:3), and Saul of Tarsus a.k.a. Paul several years later (Acts 9:1ff, I Corinthians 15:5ff, and several other places where Paul recounts the event). Acts 1:3 specifically states that Jesus appeared many times over forty days, in many different circumstances and situations to many different people and groups and types of groups, and speaks of "many convincing proofs", that He made a point of demonstrating that He was indeed alive.

other miracles are recorded. While it is relatively easy to dismiss any one account as that of a confused witness, dismissing them all as resulting from confused eyewitness accounts is a clear indication of *a priori* prejudice, that the investigator has already concluded that the events did not happen and is seeking a basis for discounting the evidence supporting them.

Finally, though, it is peculiar in an almost conspiratorial way that up until a few decades ago eyewitness testimony was accorded the highest credibility, and the doubt cast on the New Testament documents was based entirely on the assertion that they were not eyewitness accounts and so lacked that credibility. As the evidence has grown that the New Testament documents are the eyewitness accounts they claim to be, the argument has shifted to assert that eyewitness accounts are themselves unreliable. Certainly there is evidence that eyewitness accounts can be unreliable. Yet the sheer number of witnesses and the variety of events and situations reported itself demonstrates the reliability of the reports. Put another way, it is as difficult to claim that all of the reports are flawed as to claim that all are fully reliable. Taken simply as historical records, the New Testament documents demonstrate the credibility of eyewitness testimony by the number of individual accounts and witness statements incorporated.

Prophecy

I admit that I have always felt that more was made of the prophetic predictions of Jesus' life and death than the evidence would support. On the other hand, its value is not negligible.

One of the flaws is that in some cases predictions are open to some degree of interpretation. A good example is in Matthew 1:23, which quotes Isaiah 7:14 as saying that a "virgin" would conceive and bear a son. That is a valid reading of that verse in Isaiah, and indeed is exactly the way the Septuagint gives the verse.[62] However, it is already an interpretation, as although the Septuagint uses a word that unmistakably means "virgin", the Hebrew word literally means "girl", that is, a young woman, and only implies virginity from the probability that a young girl would be a virgin. The tense of the Hebrew verb is also unclear, as it might mean that she will become pregnant or it might mean only that she already is. Many Jewish scholars believe that this was a prediction that the king himself would father a son, or discover that he had fathered one, and that the name "God with us" did not mean that the son was God with us, but that the birth of the son proved that "God is with us".[63] That does not mean that

---

[62] The Septuagint is somewhat analogous to the King James Version, a translation of the Hebrew Old Testament into Greek over a century before Jesus was born which for hundreds of years was regarded the most accurate and authoritative translation for anyone who did not read Hebrew.

[63] Hebrew and Greek both allow the use of implied equations, such that the words "John the King" could mean "This is John, the king", "John is the King", "Is John the King", or "the King is John". Thus the words "God with us" could mean "This is

Matthew is wrong to apply the quote here, or that Christians have been wrong in believing that the virgin birth was predicted by Isaiah; it rather means only that we can see from the fulfillment that this is what was predicted. It can as easily be argued that this was predicting something else—and many of the predictions connected to Jesus by those who point to prophecy are like that, that they could have been predicting something else but also fit with what we know of Jesus' life. This is so prevalent that some theologians assume a double fulfillment, that predictions made by prophets were often fulfilled one way during or just after their own lives and another way centuries later in the life of Jesus.

It also bothers me that some of these supposed predictions might not have been fulfilled. Some will cite Isaiah 50:6, which among other things asserts that the speaker allowed his abusers to pull the hair from his face. We are thus told that when Jesus was arrested the soldiers pulled His beard, ripping the hair from his face. It certainly might be so, as it fits with what we know from the accounts—but the accounts do not mention it. Granted that much of what Isaiah says in chapter 50 fits as a description of what happened to Jesus, we cannot argue that the beard was torn from His face in fulfillment of prophecy demonstrating that prophecy was fulfilled, because we have no statement that asserts the fulfillment.

In these ways the prophetic claim is exaggerated.[64] However, it is still a strong claim.

God with us", or could mean "God is with us".

[64] The argument further loses credibility when those who advance it assert the probability that any one person would

The predictions of a deliverer were so strong in the Old Testament that there were denominations of Judaism divided largely on what they believed about that deliverer. In advance of the New Testament age, Old Testament scholars were certain someone was coming.

Nor can these predictions be dismissed entirely as coincidental. Psalm 22 is a remarkable example.

---

fulfill all the predictions connected to Jesus. This calculation assumes that everything predicted either would or would not happen, an even chance, then counts the number of things that did happen, uses that as a power of two, and comes up with the odds in essence of that many consecutive coin flips. There are multiple obvious problems with this mathematically. First, considering the part about whether a maiden or a virgin conceives, if we take it to be a maiden, that is, a young woman, the tendency for mothers to be young in the ancient world was high enough that we can say it is above ninety percent probable that the mother of any given individual was a young woman; however, there being no other known case of a virgin conceiving, the probability of any particular individual having a virgin mother is negligible absent a miracle or scientific intervention. Similarly, on the list of prophetic fulfillments is the fact that Jesus entered Jerusalem on the foal of a donkey. If He did so specifically to fulfill the prophecy, the probability of Him doing so is significantly higher. Dorothy Sayers suggests that there was some other reason for Him to have done so, that perhaps it was an agreed signal to someone concerning His intentions; that we do not know this makes it much more difficult to assess the probability that this would have been fulfilled. At the same time, some of the cited prophetic statements are not, in their original context, obviously identifying a future Messiah, and were we attempting to find such statements in the Old Testament we might adduce some which Jesus did not, or did not yet, fulfill. It is simple enough to say that those were not prophecies of the Messiah, or that they were prophecies of the Second Coming, but if we are trying to determine the probability that one person would fulfill all of the prophecies and we are excluding those which the one person in question did not fulfill (or which, as

Examined in detail, it describes the suffering of someone crucified, including the nails driven through the extremities, the overwhelming thirst, and more. Jesus Himself then called attention to this passage while he was dying that kind of death, when He shouted its opening words, "My God, my God, why have You forsaken me?" in Aramaic.[65] There are hundreds of events predicted in the Old Testament which are easily identified with moments in the life and death of Jesus. Certainly there are predictions which have not yet occurred (those related to the peaceable kingdom, for example), and those which we cannot know whether or not they occurred (the beard ripping), but a strong case can be made that these prophets were talking about Jesus in much of what they predicted, and that Jesus fulfilled a tremendous number of such predictions.

Put another way, if you already accepted that these prophets (who predicted events in their immediate future such as the outcomes of military invasions and the comings of famines and droughts) were predicting the coming of someone important, it would be difficult to argue that their predictions did not fit the coming of Jesus. Further, given the facts that these predictions were made centuries in advance of the events and that the Hebrew text in which they were recorded has been preserved since then by Jews who did not accept the claim that He fulfilled them, it cannot be asserted that the predictions were back-written to support the fulfillments. While we might argue individually as to which predictions were specifically about a

---

with the beard ripping, we do not know were fulfilled), we have rigged the math.

[65] Matthew 27:46; Mark 15:34.

coming deliverer in the future, enough would be found that point to such an individual and fit the life of Jesus as to make it at least likely that He was the person predicted.

Poetic Symmetry

This is an argument to which I cannot do justice, but it seems to be the argument that ultimately persuaded C. S. Lewis, and so I cannot omit it. It is less a logical argument and more a perceptual one, and as such you might easily reject it as not really proving anything. Yet in a backwards way, it seems to prove everything.

What Lewis noticed (I do not know if someone else observed it first) is that the New Testament account of Jesus fits into the history of the world in such a way that it makes sense of thousands of other otherwise disconnected bits of information. This in some ways extends the argument from prophecy: it argues that in the same way that the prophets of the Old Testament were preparing Israel for the coming of Christ and that coming then made sense of their history prior to that, so too the rest of the world was being prepared for this same event, and it also made sense of mythologies and cultures everywhere.

Cultural anthropologists will note that most cultures have a divinity modeled on the "Corn King", the one that dies and returns to life and so gives us the mythology of seeds being buried and springing up as crops. The chief exception to this is the Jews, who have only one God, a God Who is not a Corn King. Into that void comes Someone Who claims to be that God, who follows the model of the Corn King by dying and returning to life, but who never presses the idea. Suddenly all the mythologies of Corn Kings are not disconnected stories based on the same idea, but become types of the reality, the one who actually does, in a specific time and place, die and rise.

Similarly, all the mythologies of gods having children with mortal women come into focus as a virgin conceives and gives birth to a son; yet the myth is turned on its head, because that act was not of a passionate deity lusting after a beautiful woman but of a thoughtful deity implanting His child in a surrogate mother;[66] and that son is not a great warrior but a teacher and man of peace and love who helps people in need, who is ultimately executed and makes no effort to defend Himself. He is not Heracles or Perseus, but a sacrificial lamb.

Then we have all the moral codes of the world, from Hamurabi and Moses, in the East and the North and the West and the South, by any one of which most of us would be found guilty of some

---

[66] The exact biological role of Mary in the conception of Jesus is not explained to our satisfaction, in part because it was beyond the science of physiology of the time, and in part because it was not important. Some believe that Mary is the genetic mother of Jesus, and that this is important because it connects Him genetically to David, Judah, and Adam, thus making Him fully human and fully the heir of King David. Others perceive Mary more as a surrogate, that God implanted a zygote in her uterus which was fully human because He, the creator of humans, created it so, and that it is sufficient that Mary carried the child to term, delivered Him, and nursed and raised Him. The latter view is probably closer to the understanding of the time, in that at least among the Jews procreation was perceived as men planting seeds in the metaphoric soil of women; the recognition that mothers also contributed to the nature of the child beyond the quality of soil and the contributions to raising him came much later. That, though, does not resolve the question—and the answer probably is that if we do not know it probably does not matter. My description of Mary as a "surrogate" is not intended to express an opinion on the subject, but only to elucidate the absence of sexual involvement in the event.

crime; and here we find someone who announces not that those laws do not matter but that there is mercy, clemency, forgiveness for those who seek it. We stood condemned, no matter who we were or where we were, with no hope; none of us ever lived up even to our own moral or ethical code without seriously revising it after the fact. Hope is offered. It is not that nothing is really wrong, but that we are right about being guilty, but have been offered a plea bargain to escape punishment.

In ways like this, the birth, life, teaching, death, and resurrection becomes the central act of the play, turning all of history into a single unified story instead of a collection of disparate disjointed events.

Some will argue that of course the universe, having come together entirely by chance, is a collection of disparate disjointed events, and history reflects that. However, that is a personal preference, a choice to believe that everything is meaningless rather than to accept the single event that gives it all meaning.

Love Is All We Need

This isn't really proof, either, but it's somewhat compelling—or maybe it's just compelling because I was in grade school in the sixties when society exploded. What the counterculture of the time promoted, at just about every level, was that we needed to rebuild society based on love. That was the heart of the hippie movement, but it was also the core of the civil rights movement, that we were all brothers and needed to embrace each other as such. If we were going to "get back to the garden", enter "the age of Aquarius", or whatever phrase we used, we were going to do it by learning to love each other.

That, of course, was the message of Christianity. In fact, Paul's statement that there is neither Jew nor Greek cut across one of the most powerful racial barriers in all of history; that there is neither slave nor freeman similarly rejected economic barriers; that there is neither male nor female was a declaration against gender discrimination. Obviously the church did not get it all right, and sometimes did not get any of it right; but the message was always there. So was the call to love our neighbors as ourselves, even to love our enemies.

The problem with love is that it creates vulnerability. If I open my life to you, I give you power to hurt me; and the more practically I express that love, as in sharing my food, my home, my money, my self, the more power I give you. There is plenty of good solid logic, ample practical wisdom, against such love as a path in life. The way of self-preservation is self-interest; love leads to pain.

The hippies did not, I think, understand that. They had a rather selfish conception of love, that they (or many of them) were really preaching that everyone should love them, not that they would show self-sacrificial love toward everybody else. Whether that is an accurate assessment, we sometimes miss that Jesus preached the same message the right way, that we ought to love no matter what it cost us, and that He demonstrated this aspect of love at any cost by paying a terrible price. His message calls us to do the same, to sacrifice for others; and it gives us the freedom to do so, because it promises that there is nothing we can lose in this life, including life itself, that is worth keeping, because every good thing in this life will still be ours in the next. It is not "pie in the sky by and by"; it is the knowledge that we are loved, that we live in that love and show that love here and now and there and then.[67]

What I'm saying is that from the point of view of creating the perfect society, it is only created by everyone loving each other sacrificially, which means everyone taking the risk that someone will selfishly serve himself at the expense of everyone else; meanwhile from the point of view of living the best life here on earth each individual is best served by rejecting such a sacrificial attitude and selfishly

---

[67] It is interesting that the hippie counterculture became the birthplace of the Jesus Movement, perhaps the biggest Christian revival of the twentieth century. I was not present at its inception, but it may well be that those who were seeking what the hippie movement promised and failed to deliver recognized that the gospel of Jesus Christ had made the same offer, and that on some level it delivered.

seeking his own advantage. We thus are stuck with this conflict, that for the sake of the world we should love and give and for the sake of ourselves we should compete and take. The gospel breaks the dilemma, because it removes the cost of love, putting losses here into perspective as minor expenses from an infinite fortune. It makes it possible for the life of love to be the rational, even selfish, choice. That foolishness we mentioned in the *Introduction* becomes divine wisdom, because we can sacrifice our own interests, even our own lives, knowing that it is a small price for us to pay to make their lives better.

It thus fits into our notion of what the world is like and what it ought to be like, allowing us to treat it as it ought to be. In this way, too, it makes a kind of poetic sense, fitting into the world in an unexpected, unpredictable, and yet perfect way.

<u>Synchronicity</u>

A word must be said about one more evidence that is suggestive of the existence of God, not because it has had much influence on me but because it has impacted others in the twentieth century; it is said to have significantly influenced the beliefs of Albert Einstein. Carl Jung named it *Synchronicity*, and attempted to study it. Most people consider it to be coincidence, but it involves the occurrence of coincidental events at rates that defy probabilities to the point that an "a-causal connection" seems to be involved. A few popular examples will help explain it.

Whenever physicist Wolfgang Pauli was present in any laboratory, equipment would break despite the fact that he was not using it. It was common enough that it became known as the "Pauli Effect", and Otto Stern reportedly banned Pauli from his institute to protect the equipment from such malfunctions. It is reported on one occasion that a piece of equipment broke, and the experimenter actually looked to see whether Pauli was present, then wrote to him to report it as a humorous anecdote only to receive the reply that at the moment reported Pauli was on a train stopped in the station not far from the lab.

One psychiatrist reported having a patient who at seven years old had survived a fire that destroyed her home, who complained that wherever she went fires started inexplicably. He thought it a delusion, and was preparing to treat it as such at their first session when the candle he kept burning on his mantle exploded and poured burning wax down over the fireplace. Insisting it was a coincidence he scheduled her for the next week, when during their session the fire department responded to an alarm at the building across the street; again the following week as they neared the end of the session talking about her feelings from the fire, a vehicle waiting at the intersection, apparently a new van, burst into flame.

Emile Deschamps is said to have had an experience involving plum pudding. He was introduced to it by a stranger named de Fontgibu, and thereafter whenever he found it on a menu or at a private party anywhere in his travels throughout Europe, de Fontgibu would appear, a guest at the party or a patron at the restaurant. It was always unexpected and always surprised him; on one occasion he had seen the pudding listed on the menu and looked around the restaurant, then while he was explaining to his companion about the weird coincidence of the man appearing whenever he encountered plum pudding, de Fontgibu entered.

One researcher reported having ordered a vegan salad at a diner and then internally wishing he had ordered a cheeseburger and fries instead, only to have the waitress, much to the surprise of his companions, bring him the cheeseburger, certain that that was what he had ordered.

Some believe that this demonstrates something beyond the material world we can observe, and thus that there must be something like a god. Jung and Pauli referred to the *Unus Mundus*, "One World", to suggest that everything was somehow connected apart from ordinary causality, that everyone was embedded in an orderly framework of which each is the focus.

The problem is that it does not really prove anything. Empiricists of Hume's ilk would argue that highly improbable strings of coincidental events happen all the time, and that it is perfectly logical that we would sometimes observe them. The odds of being dealt an ace high straight flush in spades (Ace-King-Queen-Jack-Ten) in five card stud are something just shy of four in ten million, and yet because so many people play so many hands of poker it happens. The odds of those previously described events occurring as reported are incredibly unlikely, but nothing impossible has happened, we only have the unlikely. There is also the aspect that once we believe something to be true (or false) we tend to recall the data that supports our belief and forget that which does not—studies have demonstrated that there is no increase in craziness when the moon is full, but emergency services personnel believe it: any crazy night with a full moon encourages the belief, and any quiet full moon or crazy night that is not a full moon is ignored as an anomaly. Synchronicity has not been demonstrated to be other than remarkable coincidence that must happen given the number of events occurring simultaneously; in its very nature it cannot be shown to be otherwise, because by definition it rules out detectable cause.

On the other hand, there is enough evidence for it that people are looking for answers. Some attempt to connect it to quantum entanglement, to suggest that because it is possible for subatomic particles to become associated over long distances it is possible for that entanglement to cause related events in the larger world. No mechanism for this connection from the micro to the macro has been proposed.

Others believe that these are evidence of parapsychological phenomena, that our brains are causing fires and breakdowns, summoning friends and sending telepathic messages, outside our knowledge or control. Many people are persuaded that something is happening in these extreme coincidences; what is uncertain is exactly what that is.

The existence of a supernatural realm populated by beings quietly manipulating the natural world is a possible explanation. Some will say that this amounts to attributing to God all events not understood by us, and that is a valid objection. There might be a paranatural explanation, or a quantum explanation, or no explanation at all— people do see patterns in things which recur, because our minds are geared to find patterns.[68] On the other hand, if there is a supernatural world manipulating the natural in subtle ways, this would be the kind of event we might anticipate from it. It does not prove God, but it fits with a conception of reality predicated on His existence better than it

---

[68] A similar problem is found in the occasional pictures of the face of Jesus, when people either saw then photographed or photographed then recognized Jesus' face in melting snow or clouds or grilled cheese sandwiches. In themselves these events are unremarkable; the human mind is geared to identify patterns and particularly faces. (It is why recent anti-counterfeiting efforts have focused on putting larger pictures of people on bills, as ordinary users would not notice differences in fancy scrollwork but would immediately react to something wrong in a familiar face.) What makes these pictures worth mentioning is not that they appear but that they usually appear to someone during despair or despondency, often after prayer for comfort or reassurance. Thus we can discount the fact *that* they occur, but must account for *when* and *where*.

does in a purely materialist conception of random events.

It is a small point, but added to the rest it supplements a very significant amount of evidence favoring the existence of God and the divinity of Jesus Christ.[69]

---

[69] Einstein is quoted as having said, "Coincidence is God's way of remaining anonymous," which may have been expressing this notion that synchronicity suggests the involvement of a deity working outside our knowledge.

Arguments

Someone will now say, "But...." Something
will be said that is thought to negate all the reasons
for believing.

My first reaction to such arguments is that in the
main they are not sincere. As someone has said,
"Men do not reject the Bible because it contradicts
itself but because it contradicts them;"[70] in the same
way, most objections to theism and specifically to
Christianity are not the real reasons the objectors do
not believe, but the smokescreens, the excuses they
raise to permit themselves the luxury of disbelief.
Yet some of those objections are cogent, even when
raised by people to whom they do not matter, so
they need to be addressed. After all, someone will
say, "How can you be a Christian, given this?"
where "this" is one of these reasons. Thus it is
important to explain why these objections do not
seem critical to me. Of course, the primary reason is
that I think the evidence for the divinity of Jesus
very compelling, and at some point the answer is, I
know whom I have believed and am persuaded that
He is just and loving, even if I do not always
understand as He does. Yet there are other good
reasons specific to individual objections which
should be mentioned.

---

[70] This appeared on a sign on the library checkout desk at
Gordon College; the attribution read "Anonymous".

Suffering

God apparently allows suffering in the world. People experience pain, sometimes severe pain, sometimes for what seems a long time. No one enjoys pain for itself.[71] Could we not do without pain?

We have rare examples in the world of people who cannot feel pain, and it is a very unsafe condition. Such people are in danger of being wounded and bleeding to death, or dying of infection, simply because they are unaware that they have been harmed. Pain is thus a signal to us, alerting us that we need attention. Very few people who consider the matter would really want to be entirely without this significant warning system.

What they would like, though, is the ability to shut it down, or at least temper it, reduce it so it is not so, well, painful. To this there are several answers. The last answer probably makes the best starting point for the others. We have the ability to shut it down; we use drugs. We have developed a great variety of medications that interfere with pain in several distinct ways, and thus we can reduce and sometimes eliminate it.

It will be objected that this is a very modern development, that even a century ago we did not

---

[71] Someone will no doubt suggest that masochists enjoy pain. It is not the pain they enjoy. Rather, they have somehow gotten their connections confused such that they associate someone inflicting pain on them with someone caring about and for them, so that the pain causes them to feel desired and valuable even while it hurts and insults them. The punisher might say that the masochist is a worm not worthy of dirt, but apparently cares enough to say that.

have all these drugs, and that is certainly true; but we did have some of these drugs. Alcohol and opium have been in use to reduce pain for millennia. That we have gotten better does not mean that we did not have this ability until recently, only that we have improved on it.

It will then be objected that these are human efforts to reduce pain; why did God not do something about it? This is why it was easier to begin with the last answer. Nearly every drug we use to counter pain emulates or stimulates chemical activities already happening in the body. Our drugs are modeled on what the body is already doing for itself, either by stimulating the release of such chemicals or duplicating their structure so as to have similar effect. It was already part of the human design, that once we felt pain we would start lessening the amount of pain so we could function through it.

Yes, but this pain reduction is imperfect. Why can we not eliminate pain entirely, immediately? We felt the pain; we know there is a problem; we will deal with it later, if only the pain will subside and allow us to function on what we are doing now. That sounds promising, but it is a flawed notion.

Have you ever known anyone with a toothache, who preferred to suffer with it than face a dentist? Oral topical analgesics to reduce mouth pain are a popular over-the-counter item, and some people will use these to reduce pain until the pain stops, and never get treated. Children who could turn off their pain sense would almost certainly do so any time they were injured or sick, and so not alert adults to their need for treatment; and you do not have to be a child to believe that if it no longer hurts it is not a problem. Doctors frequently express the concern that if a patient is completely relieved of particular kinds of pains, he may overstress the injury worsening it.

Sometimes it does not work perfectly; sometimes people suffer pain that is not easily reduced for illnesses or injuries that are not easily addressed. Yet to ask why the system is imperfect is to ask why people are injured at all, and that is a much different question than asking why being injured causes pain. Pain proves to be a good thing which sometimes works ill; but that is true of nearly every good thing in life, and is hardly a fatal accusation against something that is so useful as to be pragmatically necessary.

Disaster

There is right now the aftermath of a disaster somewhere in the world. Red Cross, Salvation Army, World Vision, Feed the Children, and other organizations and agencies are bringing relief to people displaced by something—floods, hurricanes, tornadoes, earthquakes, tsunamis, blizzards, volcanic eruptions, and fires are among the more dramatic ones, but droughts, famines, and epidemics are also on the list. If God is good, why does nature attack us thus? Beyond that, we have what we might call the artificial disasters—from buildings that collapse due to age and deterioration to bombings and violence to open warfare.

Fresh from college, I took a job with a firm that contracted security services to companies, and was assigned to a fiberglass factory. I met several Christians there. I also, in my rounds, heard many conversations among both labor and management, and became aware of a number of problems. The biggest was a concern that the blast furnace which produced the glass was going to have to be shut down (it operated constantly) and rebuilt, as it was showing signs of deterioration. Yet there were budgets to be met, and during the month or so that the furnace was down there would be no way to pay the bills, no work for most of the employees. Management kept postponing the rebuild another month, another month, another month. Then my company lost the contract, and I was no longer there —but one of the employees lived a block from me, so I still heard some of what was happening there. There were tensions; there was a strike and a lockout. All the Christians that I knew left the facility for jobs elsewhere, all for different reasons. Then, during the lockout when armed security was keeping union workers away from the building, the furnace collapsed. Molten glass poured out, warping steel framing. It was a disaster—but one in which, reportedly, no one was hurt.

John Wenham in his book *The Goodness of God*[72] suggests that natural disasters are only disasters because people are in the way. Forest fires are a wonderful example of a natural event which is part of the natural growth cycle of forests, which become disasters because people have built homes they will not quickly abandon. He notes that if we knew when and where all the disasters were going to happen, we would simply move elsewhere for the time and return when the area was safe; and if we were fully attuned to the natural order (and to God) we would know this and could avoid such disasters. We could even avoid personal accidents and disasters, because God who knows the future could prepare us in the present.

While there is merit to that, it is of course irrefutable that such disasters do as much damage to churches, along with the hospitals and clinics and schools and care centers that churches operate, in short, to Christians, as to anyone else. It would of course be blatantly obvious otherwise. We are told in Luke 21:20ff that Jesus warned the disciples so that they could avoid the destruction of Jerusalem in 70 A.D., but in most cases either He has not told His followers of imminent disasters or we were not listening.

---

[72] London: Intervarsity Press, 1974.

It seems likely that both of those are true, and both are objections that have multiple answers which relate also to other objections.

One of the tropes of suspense drama is the communication failure. Someone is aware that someone else is in danger, that the villain is approaching or the area is unsafe or the bomb is about to explode, but the person who is in danger has turned off his phone or radio or removed his earpiece or in some way has made it so that he cannot be contacted. It could be very like that, that God is trying to warn us of impending danger but we are not listening, or unable to hear. Were we listening, we could prepare ourselves for whatever is about to happen.

Why, though, would God not warn His people of an impending disaster, that they could prepare, perhaps move out of the way, perhaps save others from it? There is a point, that God chooses not to be obvious, which we ultimately will address; for the moment, that fact itself will have to suffice. Yet there is also a degree to which pain and suffering and disaster are necessary for God's purpose. Not to delve into it too deeply, that discussion about God teaching us to love each other is very much central to why we are here, and why the world is the way it is. Love requires risk; risk requires the potential for loss or pain. If there were no loss or pain, there would be no risk; if there were no risk, love would not cost anything and there would be no particular value in it. Love matters precisely because there is the possibility of pain for the one who loves, and for the one loved who is soothed by that love. If it cost nothing, it would mean nothing.

It is thus certainly true that disasters create opportunities for those unaffected by the disaster to show love by aiding those suffering. This is the kind of caring love for people we have come to expect, thanks originally to Christian charities like the Salvation Army[73] and ultimately secular groups such as the Red Cross following their lead. Those groups and the people who support them have a tremendous impact on the wounded. Yet this sort of kindness is even more dramatic when it comes from people similarly hit by the disaster. If I, a thousand miles away, go through my larder and ship food that I will replace on my next trip to the store and probably won't miss before that, it has cost me a very small amount; but if I have just lost as much as you, but I have a few salvaged bits of food and I am willing to share them with you instead of hoarding them for myself, I have demonstrated the kind of self-sacrifice that love truly involves. I cannot actually do that, nor even know whether I would do it, without disasters which impact me as much as you. The story of the widow who gave the tiny bit that was the last of her money, contrasted against the wealthy men who lavished large quantities of surplus cash,[74] is very much about this, that it is easy to give when you have plenty, but the true expression of giving, of love, comes when you in rational terms cannot afford it but choose to do so anyway.

---

[73] The Salvation Army is of course a relatively modern example. Organized and spontaneous charitable Christian help dates back centuries.
[74] Mark 12:41ff, Luke 21:1ff.

God does not send or cause disasters, but He has created a world in which they occur in order that we might better learn to express love for others, both when we are not suffering and when we are.

Evil

Pain and disaster have been addressed. They could have been treated as subheadings under a section of why there is evil in the world, but it may be easier to discuss the rather abstract notion of "evil" having first removed those two concrete expressions of it. People suffer; sometimes the suffering is due to what we might dismiss as accidental causes—being in the wrong place at the wrong time. Sometimes, though, injury is inflicted intentionally.

On consideration, though, it appears that evil is a natural and necessary possibility of freedom. If we ask why God did not create a world in which no one could harm anyone, we find that it gives us a world in which either no one can choose what to do at all, or no one can meaningfully help anyone else either. When a man was beaten, robbed, and left alongside the road, before a Samaritan appeared to help him two others passed on the other side of the road.[75] Their crime was simply that they did not help, and in choosing not to help they caused harm. A world in which we are compelled always to do good and never to do evil is not a free world, and not a world in which we can truly learn to love, because there is no alternative.

Yes, but could God not have limited the evil that happens in this world? We do not know whether He could have created a world in which we have free choice and also limited how much evil we could do. We do not even know with any certainty that He did not do exactly that.

---

[75] Luke 10:30ff.

In the wake of World War II, the Soviet Union developed its own nuclear weapons program to balance ours. This led to a policy called M.A.D., which stood for Mutually Assured Destruction. It was sometimes dubbed the Balance of Terror, and it was believed that no one would dare start a world war because the consequences were too horrifying. Thus there were wars all over the world through which the United States and the Soviet Union fought each other by proxy, each providing military support to one side against the other, and it never escalated. This is the more surprising, perhaps, because prior to World War I there was a similar concept dubbed the Balance of Powers. In essence, every major developed country in the western world was allied with other countries through mutual defense treaties, such that if any one country were attacked half the "civilized" world would be obligated to come to its aid against the other half of the "civilized" world, and such a war was unthinkable, and therefore no one would dare start it. There was someone, though, who perhaps did not know, perhaps did not care, perhaps did not believe that such a war would occur, and so it was triggered. There was no reason to believe that M.A.D. would work any better. Yet it did. Ultimately the Cold War ended without a single nuclear attack despite the many fictional accounts that predicted how it would happen.

We do not know and cannot say that God did not permit a nuclear war; even if we believe He did, that does not necessarily mean that He will not permit one in the future. At the same time, we cannot say that God has not put limits on the evil that men can do. We simply do not know.

That there are terrible evils in the world is not at all compelling, because apart from horror stories we have no real concept of how terrible it might be, and thus very little basis for comparison. If we lived in a nearly perfect world in which the worst that ever happened was the occasional hangnail, someone would ask why God permits the horror that is a hangnail. We have no zombies or vampires, no alien invaders, and while scientific reasons for the absence of these things might be advanced, that would not make their non-existence any less a divine limitation if indeed it is. It is something of a proof conundrum: if the thing cannot exist for reasons of the design of the universe, then saying God did or did not limit it depends on whether you believe God designed it; if it could exist or happen and simply has not to this point (or did not at some point), then either the limitation is arbitrary or it is not actually a limitation. That is, we do not know whether God will prevent global thermonuclear war, only that it has not yet happened; to test whether God is preventing it we would have to attempt to start it, and were we to succeed all we would prove is that God did not prevent it. There is no way of demonstrating whether God is limiting evil, because there is no way to know what limits there might be.

Poverty

It is asked how God can allow such abject
poverty as we often see, and have seen over the
centuries. Nothing is more heart-wrenching than
that children starve, and God does nothing about it.

This, though, is not God's fault; it is our fault. It
appears that the resources available on the earth are
sufficient to feed all its people—despite the fact that
there are many times more people now than there
were in previous centuries. We waste food; we
destroy food; we pay farmers not to grow it so as to
support prices that will adequately recompense those
farmers. We arm our borders against starving
refugees so we will not have to share our wealth
(and food is the ultimate wealth). We could feed
everyone in the world; we simply choose not to do
so. Part of it is greed, that we want to keep the
abundance for ourselves, and that if we are going to
part with our food we want those who receive the
food, who of course have nothing of their own to
offer in trade, to owe us, to pay us for the food we
have. Certainly it is unfair for a few to have to work
in order for others who do not work to be able to eat;
it is also unfair to hoard food simply because those
who are starving have nothing to offer in exchange.
Part of it, too, is laziness, that delivering the food to
the starving is work someone has to do, and we do
not wish to do it. We could pay someone else to do
it, but then our greed comes back into the picture, as
we would rather spend our resources on our own
comforts and pleasures than pay for someone else to
eat.

We expect this selfishness of others, and excuse it in ourselves; but we cannot blame God for failing to feed the hungry we make no effort to feed.

It is wrong, of course, to say that we make no effort. Major organizations previously mentioned work to bring food and other aid to the destitute and impoverished; government organizations do the same in tax and welfare systems. People are making an effort, and making more of an effort now than ever before. Hunger and poverty are being reduced, and against the odds as world population is increasing rapidly. The church has done this repeatedly throughout history, and other groups (many founded by Christians originally) have taken up the task. We will always have the poor—Jesus said that, too[76]—but that is part of giving us opportunities to help others.

It also opens another question.

---

[76] Matthew 26:1, Mark 14:7, John 12:8.

Crusades

It is certainly not just the Crusades, but they are the most frequently mentioned example of Christians behaving badly. The Inquisition is also sometimes mentioned. It is more difficult to find examples in modern times, not because they do not exist but because they are harder to define. For example, in Latin America in the mid twentieth century Roman Catholic bishops tended to support the oppressive right-wing governments while Roman Catholic clergy tended to support the left-wing Marxist revolutionary movements. We from the outside could condemn both movements, but the region was notoriously short on moderates at the time, and if you supported no one you either went unnoticed or were quietly eliminated by one side or the other. Certainly there were Christian Nazi collaborators; there were also many Christians working against the Nazis, many of whom were interred in concentration camps.[77] In the midst of the conflict it is not as easy to identify right and wrong sides as it is from the outside or in hindsight. Throughout history Christians have died in the defense of the weak; just as persistently there have been Christians among the oppressors.

Gandhi rejected Christianity not on its merits but on the merits of those who claimed to be its adherents. He was only half right. There have been some in history who have lived considerably more closely to what Jesus taught than most of those whom he could observe in colonial India. One

---

[77] More non-Jews died under Nazi purges than Jews; what is notable about the Jews is that a greater percentage of an identifiable group was targeted.

wonders what he would have thought had he known Saint Teresa of Calcutta. The majority of those claiming the name "Christian" fail, many of us horribly so.

It is tempting to say that many of those were not true Christians. This winds up being the "no true Scotsman" fallacy, that we begin by saying no member of the group would do anything like this, then define the group by excluding anyone who does. It might help to note that Jesus more than once commented that there would be people claiming to be His followers who were not (most dramatically in the parable of the sheep and the goats),[78] but it does not fall to me to make those distinctions, and whatever I think about their conduct, I must accept that anyone claiming to be Christian is, at least from the perspective of those condemning Christianity, one of us.

More significantly, nothing about Christianity says that Christians would be perfect. It promises to make any given Christian better than he would have been had he not been a Christian, which is of course something we cannot estimate or demonstrate. It means that we are fallible, we can be deceived and misled and used by others with a good line and an agenda. We can misunderstand our own purpose, our own calling, our own faith. We are not immune to being wrong.

On the modern stage it is again more complicated. Many Christians take particular positions on modern issues, and those who disagree with them accuse them of failing to be what they ought to be. The twentieth century conflicts in Latin America are a safe example, as all over the world

---

[78] Matthew 25:31ff.

there were people who thought that opposing the established oppressive governments was supporting anarchy and left-wing military dictatorships that would (and sometimes did) arise, while at the same time there were those who believed that supporting those same governments was opposing the freedom and human rights of the peasants. Those who think that Christians are wrong because they take a position on some present political, social, or moral issue need to consider whether this makes the Christians wrong or whether it might be possible that they themselves, as objectors, are on the wrong side of the issue. Often all the defined "sides" in an issue are wrong in some way. Even if on reflection you conclude that your position is the correct one, that does not make your opposition wicked or uncaring or immoral or hateful for believing that they are correct. Some will make wrong choices; some might be swept into wrong beliefs and actions by a failure to grasp the truth. That happens not merely to Christians but to humans, and it is very difficult as a human to know whether you have been swept into a political, social, or moral opinion that fails to recognize a basic truth, at least until you recognize that truth.

Agnosticism

Some object that it is impossible for a finite creature, man, to reason his way to understanding an infinite creator, God, and therefore we cannot know whether or not God exists, or anything about Him.

I am somewhat inclined to agree with this. The very concept of God includes that He would be incomprehensible in so many ways; we could never reason our way to understanding what He is like. It is hopeless; we cannot discover God, and so it would seem that we cannot know Him.

That is, we would not be able to know Him were it not for the concept of revealed religion: we cannot find our way to God, but He can easily introduce Himself to us. That is what Judaism claims, and what Christianity intensifies, that God contacted people, and revealed Himself.

The Bible rarely speaks of what individuals thought for themselves. We find some of that in Proverbs and Ecclesiastes, and perhaps in Job, although most of what men think in Job is ultimately repudiated. What we find, rather, is that God interacted with people, beginning (according to the stories) with Adam and Eve, then with Cain and Abel, and down through the generations with Enoch, Noah, Abraham and Sarah, Isaac, Jacob, Moses, Joshua, Gideon, Judith, Samuel, David, Solomon, Elijah, Elisha, Isaiah, Jeremiah, Ezekiel, Daniel, and many others; ultimately with Zechariah and Elizabeth, with Mary and Joseph, with Peter, James, John, Andrew, Matthew, Simon, Thaddeus, Bartholomew, Mary Magdalene, Martha and Mary and Lazarus, Paul, and innumerable others. He wanted to make Himself known to us, and so came to us on His terms. We could not know Him, could not discover Him, could not come to Him; but He always knew us and came to us to reveal Himself to us.

It is sometimes objected that everything we know about God is understood in metaphor—that God is light, as the sun is light; that God is a father, as we have earthly fathers. There are two aspects to this objection, the one that it follows that we have invented our idea of God from that which we know, the other that God is not really like the metaphors at all, which are inadequate to the purpose, God being entirely different from anything material or mortal.

To the first, the fact that something is like something else does not mean that either of those objects does not exist. Lamps are like the sun, but the existence of both concepts does not prove that we extrapolated the existence of a non-existent sun from seeing lamps, nor that we imagine non-existent lamps because we saw the sun. Even given that we might have invented the existence of God from these other objects and relationships, that does not demonstrate that we did so. If we knew conclusively that God did not exist, we might explain the belief in God based on such metaphoric extrapolation. However, since we do not know God does not exist, we cannot conclude from that argument that He is invented by our imaginations, any more than that we can demonstrate that the sun is an invention of our imaginations extrapolated by analogy to lamps.[79]

---

[79] I am probably indebted to C. S. Lewis for this analogy, which he used in his fictional book *The Silver Chair*, part of *The Chronicles of Narnia*, various dates and publishers in various forms and collections. In the story, the witch attempts

To the second, there are many things we cannot understand without relying on metaphor. Descriptions of the activity of electrical currents are, in the use of the very word "currents", analogized to water and air. Those who attempt to say that God is not a father then attempt to provide other descriptions, but their descriptions are also metaphors—God is no more a "force" than a "father", in the literal sense. Yet there is an aspect to the metaphors of the Bible that is overlooked by many, in two parts. The first part is that these are by and large the metaphors God used to describe Himself—the concepts of "father", "bridegroom", along with "light" and "rock", have a claim to being the best metaphors because they are those God chose. The second part, the part most often overlooked, is that when God designed the universe, He had the option to create it in ways that gave Him the metaphors He would need to explain Himself. As a writer, when I seek to express something in metaphor I have to struggle to find something that conveys my idea.[80] God had the luxury of creating objects that would provide the best metaphors to describe Himself. Thus when He identifies Himself metaphorically as a "father", not only can we conclude that His choice of the image of fatherhood is among the best available, we can also recognize

---

to bewitch the children into believing that the sun does not exist because it is like the lamps in her underground world in a way which suggests they invented the bigger lamp in their imaginations.

[80] Hopefully I have never done so poorly as the schoolboy who wrote, "The boat floated across the water exactly the way a bowling ball wouldn't."

that in creating fatherhood itself He was providing something which conveyed the desired image.

That revelation of Himself to individuals raises another issue, though, sometimes raised as an objection.

Exclusivity

It is sometimes argued that God let millions be lost while He unfairly singled out one individual. He chose Abraham, and Abraham's descendants, and let the rest of the world go to hell, perhaps quite literally.

Let's first note that we do not know what happened, in ultimate terms, to the rest of the world. We know that God chose Abraham, and we know that God claims to be fair. We also recognize that we can hardly claim Him to be unfair, because (as we saw previously in the section *The Apologies: Moral*) either He has given us our very concept of "fair" or it is not a valid concept. Whatever He did, we are not at this point in a position to claim that it was unfair.

On the other hand, there is something that is often unnoticed about this story, because it is buried in the boring parts.

It begins with the accounts of the children of Adam and Eve. I do not say that you have to accept these as accurate historical accounts; that's an entirely separate question. What you have to accept is that this is what was believed about those people at the time of Moses, and likely earlier (there are reasons to believe that the Genesis accounts were collected and redacted from writings handed down for generations from father to son and stored by Joseph in the libraries of Egypt, where Moses had access to them). What we find is that of the first three sons, the second was killed by the first, who was thus effectively banished; that means that the third son, Seth, was head of the family.

We then are given a rather dull string of "begats", that is, lists that tell us that this person had a son who was that person, and then had a bunch of other children, and then died, but that first son had a son, and so on. If we follow the line, we find that Noah was not just some individual God picked to build a boat; he was the first born son of the first born son all the way back to Seth. Given the rules of primogeniture—which have mattered through most of human history in most human cultures—Noah was the head of the human family.

We then find the same sequence coming down from Noah through another list of individuals including someone named Eber (who will matter in a moment) to Abraham, who again is the first born son of the first born son all the way back through Noah to Seth, the putative head of the human family.

We overlook this, but the Genesis account does not. At one point, Abraham is identified by the people among whom he is staying as a Hebrew[81]— that is, a descendant of Eber. It suggests that they were aware that Eber (who, if we take the lifespan information seriously,[82] was still alive) stood in the peculiar position of firstborn of the human family.

That this concept of primogeniture matters is then underscored, again missed by most even who study the Bible, by the subsequent passing of the torch. Isaac is the only child of Abraham's first wife; under the rules of primogeniture the children he had by his other wives are secondary to that. Jacob was not the firstborn, but persuaded the firstborn to sell him that position, and so made a

---

[81] Genesis 14:18.
[82] This will be addressed later, in the section on *The Fall*.

bargain to get it. Jacob's first children were Reuben, then Simeon, then Levi, then Judah; but Reuben slept with one of his father's wives,[83] and Simeon and Levi reneged on a deal their father had made with one of the princes of the land,[84] and so the three of them were all disinherited from the leadership position. That meant that primacy in the family fell to Judah, ancestor of David and of the Jews. They were not selected at random; they were selected because they were the primary inheritors of the heritage of humanity. There was nothing arbitrary about it; and if the rest of the family ignored or rejected what the family head knew, God is not to blame for that.

Beyond that, the arms of God were always open. Moses had a foreign wife;[85] David as we noted had a foreign great-grandmother.[86] There were numerous persons from foreign lands who embraced faith in the God of Israel. One took a cartload of dirt home with him, so that he could stand on the land of Israel and worship God as if there.[87]

God's work was focused on one man, one line, one people; but it was never exclusive.

---

[83] Genesis 35:22.

[84] Genesis 34; the sons in essence broke a peace treaty, killing an entire family rather than accept the peace agreement their father had made to allow their sister to become wife of the boy who raped her, and in essence undermining the trust others would place in Jacob's promises.

[85] Exodus 2:16ff.

[86] Ruth, whose story is told in the book of that name, and who is listed in the genealogy of Jesus in Matthew 1:5.

[87] II Kings 5:17.

Duality

Then there are those who object that the Christian God, the God of the New Testament, is not the Jewish God, the God of the Old Testament. This is certainly not a new claim. The heretic Marcion made it in the mid second century, editing his version of the New Testament to exclude all books or passages that suggested a connection between them.[88] We are told that the Old Testament God is legalistic, demanding, harsh, even vengeful, while the New Testament God is loving, merciful. They cannot be the same God, we are told, unless He is schizophrenic.

It cannot be said that He is not complex; at the same time, much of what is said about the Old Testament God misunderstands the Old Testament.[89] The way Paul describes it in Galatians may be the simplest way to understand it. In essence, he says that when we were young and immature, we were placed under tutelage, taught by instructors how we ought to act. Let us take a simple childhood example. When we were very young, we were probably all told, "Don't touch the stove." As adults, we understand this, and we say it to our own very young children, because sometimes the stove is

---

[88] Earlier Gnostic cults, such as the late first century Docetics (who asserted that Jesus only seemed to have a material body, since a good spirit could not be present in a form made of evil matter) held a similar view, that the god who created the universe was not the good God above all gods but some lesser spirit. We know less about them.

[89] The Jews themselves do not see their God in such a light. The work of Abraham Joshua Heschel, for example, shows a vision of God at once just and merciful, seeking to protect the weak and persecuted.

dangerous, and a very young child might not be able to distinguish when it is safe and when it is not. But that imperative morphs into, "Don't touch the stove without Mommy to help you," because we will have to learn that part about knowing when and how to touch the stove. It then becomes "Be careful when you use the stove," and then "I don't have to remind you to be careful when you use the stove," and finally the rule vanishes entirely—not because stoves become safe, but because we have grown to understand how to use this dangerous device safely.

Many Christians, even many Christian ministers, do not really understand this fundamental of the gospel message. It is given in Acts 15, when the Jewish leaders of the church discuss what to do about the gentile converts. It is driven forward in Paul's letter to the Galatians, and presented in his letter to the Romans, and scattered throughout the book. We who come to Christianity not as Jews but as gentiles, non-Jews, are told in no uncertain terms that all those rules are not for us; we do not have to obey them.[90] That's not because we are free to kill and steal and commit adultery and the rest, but because we have entered the "adult" form of the faith, in which we know that killing and stealing and committing adultery are unloving, harmful to others, and harmful to ourselves. We don't obey the rules because they are rules; we live lives that follow the way of Christ, which happen to comport with most —not all—of the rules. We still don't beat our little brother when we disagree over a toy, because we see

---

[90] The relationship of Jewish Christians to the Law is more complicated, involving their culture and history as well as promises between their ancestors and God; it is beyond the scope of this book.

that that is a bad way to resolve our disagreements. We no longer adhere to the rule of holding Mommy's hand when we cross the street, because we have (hopefully) learned to use the same care in crossing the street which Mommy used for us when we were too young to understand it.[91]

Yet we are told that the God of the Old Testament is a violent God. He ordered entire cities burned to the ground with the populations including the livestock massacred.[92] The God of the New Testament is not like that, we are told; He directs His people to turn the other cheek,[93] to exercise non-violence in all situations, to die rather than fight.

Concerning the latter, it is not strictly true. Jesus gives us the example of violently driving moneychangers and sacrifice salesmen out of the Temple for what He considered the sacrilegious profiteering on a holy act.[94] He warned His disciples

---

[91] This mature understanding of moral concepts has often been and continues to be a problem within the church. Augustine was able to say that the law of God could be summarized as, "Love God, and do as you please," but he understood that his actions would thereby be constrained by his love for God. It is relatively easy to miss this understanding, to act in ways completely out of character for a child of God; it is thus just as easy for those who recognize the flaw in such actions to respond with the statement that we should not behave so, and for simplicity it becomes codified into a new law. Yet the gospel message is as Augustine saw it, that if we truly love Christ we will want to act in ways pleasing to Him, to be as much like Christ as we can, and thus without a law we come to live in a way consistent with the law.

[92] E.g., Joshua 8:8.

[93] Matthew 5:39, Luke 6:29.

[94] Matthew 21:12ff, Mark 11:15ff, John 2:14ff. It is not merely that they were doing business in the outer court of the temple; it is that there were several ways in which they were colluding to cheat their customers. People came to bring sacrifices, and

on one occasion that they might need to carry swords,[95] and He was smart enough to know that if you carry a sword it can only be because you might have to use it—He gave us the quote, "Those who live by the sword will die by the sword."[96] Christians do not agree on all points on this—for some of us, self-defense is warranted, and for some it is not, but defense of third persons is, and for some it is better to die than to kill; but there is no

---

the expectation was that they would bring an animal from their own flocks. Not all Jews had flocks, of course, so animals were sold in the temple courtyard. Too, an animal brought on a long journey to Jerusalem was likely to have suffered along the way, and sacrificial animals were to be perfect as determined by a priest—but the priests were part of the scam, and would reject healthy animals and recommend that the worshipper buy an animal from the dealers, certified as acceptable. However, because this was the house of God, the secular money issued by that occupying force that was the Roman Empire could not be spent in the temple, so there were men who would exchange your Roman money for good Jewish temple money so you could buy a sacrifice—at a small fee, of course, because they had to make a living. Good Jewish temple money was nearly worthless outside the temple, though, where everyone used Roman money, so again the moneychangers would buy back your temple coin for Roman, again at a small fee. You then would buy your sacrifice, which you would take to the priest, who would then return it to the merchant to be sold again—sacrifices were made, and every animal purchased was ultimately sacrificed, but there were more sacrifices than could be burned in a day and no one would recognize their own animal after it had been slaughtered, so they were able to sell the same certified perfect animal multiple times at premium prices. This was what Jesus opposed. There were other Jews who objected to these practices, but the priests who controlled the temple and profited from the practice were officially recognized by Rome as a governing body in Jerusalem.

[95] Luke 22:36.

[96] Matthew 26:52.

inherent reason why Christians cannot in good conscience be in the military or the police, and use potentially lethal force in a good cause, and even accept the notion that those who give the orders have wrestled with the issues and decided that lethal force is the best option under the circumstances.[97] Part of that is because of that part about the rules not really applying—we recognize that killing is unloving and even self-destructive, and empirically that is supported in the lives of those who have had to kill as part of their military or police positions, but we also recognize that it's not a law and a good part of it is left to our judgment as adult children of God, knowing that it is a bad thing only to be done to prevent a worse one.

As to the violence of the God of the Old Testament, there are several points that should be taken into account.

The first is that we do not know all the circumstances, but the circumstances we know are suggestive. God did not drive the people out of Canaan when Abraham first arrived, nor indeed for quite a few generations thereafter, and it was not merely because there were not yet enough Israelites to hold the land. Reference is made to the notion that the people of Canaan were doing things that would have to be stopped[98]—and our archaeology has uncovered evidence of child sacrifice and child

---

[97] A distinction should be made between trusting that those giving the orders have based them on sound moral principles and reasonably reliable information, and obeying orders that are clearly wrong. An order to destroy a village that is reliably believed to be housing enemy soldiers disguised as civilians is different from an order to destroy a civilian village simply because it is in enemy territory.

[98] E.g., Genesis 15:16.

torture, and of sexual and sanitary practices that had encouraged the spread of severe infectious diseases. It was necessary that the Israelites not abandon the rather strict sexual and sanitary rules that are incorporated into that Law they were given, and that in part meant that they should be isolated from people who did not follow those rules and seemed to be fine. It was also necessary that the infections were contained, so they would not spread to Israel, either to the people or even to their livestock. We have modern means of dealing with outbreaks, including medicines, quarantines, and more; but it is noteworthy that in *The Andromeda Strain*[99] Michael Crichton's final defense against an alien plague was the nuclear destruction of the infected area. Sterilization of the area by fire was the most effective tool they had.[100]

---

[99] ©1969 Dell Publishing, New York.

[100] Some object to the seemingly loose application of the death penalty in Moses' Law; it is ordered for crimes ranging from intentional murder to disobedience to parents. Yet several points must be recognized in this. First, this law was given to a nomadic people who lived in tents. Life imprisonment was not an option ("Saul, we're moving, pack up your prison tent— Saul? Saul?"), and banishment would not be effective as the villain could always return among others who would not recognize him. The Law included some stiff evidentiary requirements (the agreement of two independent witnesses on the details) and penalties for perjury (one of the Ten Commandments). The prescribed method of execution— stoning—required that the community be in agreement on the guilt of the accused and the necessity of the punishment, as he would effectively die at their hands. Frequently the accuser had to be involved. Significant in this is that for a child to be executed for disobedience (what we would call juvenile delinquency) his own parents would have to bring the charge and participate in the execution. The commandment not to kill literally means not to commit murder, that is, it is illegal to kill

Further, He was ultimately even-handed about it. He declared that Israel was going to be victorious over the people they displaced, and for centuries over the people who attempted to displace or conquer them; but when they failed to follow Him as their God (a point made clearly in the Old Testament) He brought armies against them and removed them from the land. All of it was part of a program to make His several points clear, and when we reach the end of the Old Testament Israel knows more about God than the rest of us, because God took the time to explain Himself to them as a step toward explaining Himself to the rest of us.

So yes, God seems different in the Old Testament than in the New, by as much as our parents seemed different to us when we were infants than when we became adults. It is not He who has changed, but we.

---

anyone unlawfully; it does not exclude capital punishment, and the attitude that such executions are murder is a modern sentiment in a different world with different options. It may be that modern penology is more merciful and more just; whether it is as effective is another issue, but also a moot one given the conditions under which the Law was originally applied.

Insignificance

Some cut away all this discussion with the objection that the universe is so vast that anything that happens here could not possibly matter on a universal scale. We are told that the universe is teeming with life, and thus that this disproves the Christian message to the degree that man matters. This objection of course begins with the assumption that man does not matter, which it makes based on the observation that man is a relatively small entry in time and space.

It might be answered that man might not be the most important thing in all creation, but only has that importance that is represented by the lost sheep, the lost coin, or the prodigal son,[101] that of having the greatest need, of being that which is lost, or most lost. It then suggests that God came here, to humanity, not because there are no others in the universe as important as we are, but that there are no others in the universe in as great a need as we are.[102]

While that answer is good, I don't really believe it. My reading of Paul tells me that the redemption of the entire universe is connected to what Jesus did here on earth, and that it is so because the corruption of the entire universe arises from the fall of man. That is another issue, next on the list; what matters at this point is that the Bible seems to contend that mankind really is the center of the universe.

Let's be clear: it does not use that phrase, "center of the universe". Nor does it in any way require that we be at the physical center of the

---

[101] Luke 15.
[102] This is the way, I think, C. S. Lewis saw it; he referred to this several times in his writings.

universe—the most important parts of most stories and most musical works are near the end, and thus centrality of position and centrality of importance are not connected in any absolute or necessary way. The issue is that it appears that the arrival of God in the midst of history is the central act in history, not merely of humanity but of the universe. Further, if indeed God did arrive exactly one time in the midst of the history of the universe, that would almost certainly be the most important moment in that history, particularly since we are not talking about a Stan Lee cameo[103] but an act of redemption designed to demonstrate to the creation the love of the Creator.

I also agree with C. S. Lewis that it is highly unlikely that something like the incarnation of God happened on thousands of worlds spread throughout the universe. It cheapens the notion of the death and resurrection of Christ, if it could be repeated that way. I think that it might have been accomplished if somehow God arranged it such that Christ appeared on multiple worlds simultaneously, and suffered and died on all of them in what was in some sense a single act at a single moment in time. I can imagine it being so, but I don't think that's how it happened.

So the first problem is simply that the universe is so very big. As Lewis observes, though, while this seems to be a new problem, it's not new information. Ptolemy, second century astronomer whose *Almagest* was the standard for astronomy for centuries, stated that the universe was so vast that the planet Earth was effectively a mathematical

---

[103] It is something of an insider joke that comic creator Stan Lee appears briefly in insignificant roles in all Marvel Comics superhero movies.

point, that is, functionally having no dimensions when calculating interactions of celestial bodies. Thus for centuries every educated person knew that by relative size the Earth was insignificant, and it wasn't until very recently that anyone thought that made it unimportant.

There is also nothing logical about the notion that size correlates to importance. Buildings are not more important than people; legs are not more important than heads; boulders are not more important than grapes. We see this rather clearly when the size difference is relatively small; but if stars were more important than people because of their size, then what is true on that scale must remain true on the smaller scale, that small differences in size mean small differences in importance, but no sane person would argue that a six foot tall three hundred pound man is more important than a five foot tall one hundred pound man, not thrice as important (going by weight) nor twenty percent more important (by height), and in fact not more important because of size at all. Thus the notion that the Earth is unimportant because it is dwarfed by the size of the universe is complete nonsense, and until fairly recently has always been recognized as such. That anyone would think size was correlated with importance today is puzzling.

Some, though, argue that it is not the size of the stars which make them important but their life spans, that a star exists for billions of years. Some stars are estimated to be nearly as old as the universe itself. In contrast, all of human history is an instant in time, and the life of a man an inconsequential flash even against a relatively short-lived several-million-year-old star. Again, though, what is true in the large scale must be true in the small, and we do not think clams[104] more important than salmon,[105] or value animals based on how long they live or might live. Indeed, this notion of the importance or value of an object being connected to its longevity is extremely controversial in our time: nations live longer than men, and many totalitarian regimes base their authority on the conclusion that the nation is thus more important than the individual and has the right to control the life of the individual completely. Yet even if it were so that longevity is linked to importance, the Christian message includes the point that humans are, at least potentially, immortal, beings with an unending future. Thus the argument that we are unimportant because we are short-lived relative to celestial bodies fails because it assumes that we are short-lived, which is a conclusion drawn from the argument but a necessary presupposition to it (it assumes what it attempts to prove). If we are potentially eternal beings, we will outlive the universe, and so the argument cannot be used to prove we are not important because it cannot prove we are not eternal beings.

---

[104] The Artica Islandica or Ocean Quahog clam is reported to live from at least four hundred to over five hundred years, making it the longest-living known creature on earth.

[105] Salmon are born in fresh water, spend some time in the salt waters of the ocean, and then return to fresh water to spawn and die. Some make their return one year after they are born, and few live longer than eight years. Certainly there are creatures with shorter life spans, but there are a number of reasons why we value salmon, including their position in the food chain (eaten by many creatures including bears, eagles, and humans) and their intriguing life cycles. They are one of the few fish that live in both fresh and salt water, and of course their quest to return to their birthplaces to lay their eggs is nearly legendary.

However, we are told that the universe is, or must be, teeming with intelligent life much like ourselves, and thus that we are an unimportant accident of molecular biology and evolution. This, though, makes a number of untenable assumptions.

The first is the notion that the universe is teeming with intelligent life. It is one of those ideas that cannot be disproved and thus is useless as a theory; it also proves to be entirely circular. It asserts that because life occurred accidentally here, and because the forces that produced all the conditions required for life to occur here are found throughout the universe and the universe is so vast that there are uncountable examples of situations similar to our own, intelligent life must have happened accidentally in thousands of other places, all of which might be too far from us for us ever to find them.

There are assumptions in that math. It has long been assumed that the forces which formed our planetary system are such that most planetary systems would be like ours, with small rocky planets close to the star and gas giants farther away from it. We have now discovered a couple hundred other planetary systems, and all but one of them to this point reject the pattern; the theory is mistaken. That means that there are far fewer rocky planets in the right zone from their host star than the calculation expected.

So what? There are still millions of such planets. Indeed there are; but there are other questionable assumptions in the mix. One of those is that if a planet has the right conditions for life to occur, life will eventually occur. This is a particularly odd assumption, given that we have never been able to generate life by creating conditions in a lab and pressing those conditions in the way we think has to occur to create life. We have created some amino acids, but despite their use in biochemistry they are ultimately just chemical compounds. The creation of life might be entirely improbable; so might the development of intelligence. There are so many points in the process at which an assumption is made that because it happened here it must be probable, when all the evidence suggests that what has happened here is entirely improbable.[106] Life is the exception. It is still possible that we might be unique in the universe.[107]

For some, though, this is an argument against the inevitable. If you believe there is intelligent life beyond Earth, then you hope that evidence will be found, and perhaps expect that eventually it will be found. It is an impossible argument, though. On the one hand, if the universe is found to be teeming with

---

[106] For example, we are often told of the eons for which dinosaurs ruled the earth, many times longer than the entire history of the evolution of man, yet there is no evidence that what we consider rational intelligence appeared among them. If such a development is inevitable, why did it not happen in the nearly two hundred million years of the "Mesozoic", the "dinosaur age"?

[107] A paper entitled *Dissolving the Fermi Paradox* published June 8, 2018 by Anders Sandberg, Eric Drexler and Toby Ord of the Future of Humanity Institute, Oxford University posted by the Cornell University Library at https://arxiv.org/pdf/1806.02404.pdf reaches much the same conclusion, asserting that it is up to 85% probable that we are the only intelligent life in the observable universe, up to 99.6% that we are the only such life in our galaxy. It reaches that conclusion by considering the uncertainties in the factors used by the Drake Equation.

life but none of it is intelligent, then that is irrelevant; it proves nothing relative to whether God would choose to come to this one planet to save the universe, because we might still be unique. It will lead some to say that because we have found life somewhere outside Earth it increases the probability that it will have evolved to become intelligent somewhere else in the universe; yet the only proof that there is intelligent life outside this planet will be if we make contact with such life and, barring issues of the credibility of close encounters stories, we have not done so, and some who sincerely believe that life is out there just as sincerely believe that we never will contact anyone, which makes the issue of intelligent life elsewhere entirely a matter of speculative faith, of what you choose to believe in the absence of any evidence. There is far more evidence for the resurrection of Jesus Christ than there is for the existence of life, let alone intelligence, outside our local biosphere.

Suppose, though, that such life does exist. Would that disprove the Christian message? To answer this, we have to ask what kind of universe we expect God to create. After all, for the way the universe actually is to disprove the existence of God, we have to know what kind of universe is inconsistent with His existence.

As soon as we ask the question, we should realize that we have stepped beyond what we know. After all, we do not know that this is the only universe God created; He could have created dozens, even millions, each unique in some way. There could be universes with four, five, six, any number of spatial dimensions, and universes with multi-dimensional time. God's expression of his creativity could be limitless. If we found ourselves in a universe which seemed improbable for God to have created it, that would not prove it was not one of many, any more than finding a portrait on a seven inch canvas would prove that the artist did not also do cathedral murals, towering statues, or airplane design. We are working from the observations of a single work of the Creator without any knowledge of whatever other work He may have done. Further, the mention of created angelic beings in the Bible suggests that He has done other work. We do not have unrestricted access to His oeuvre; we do not even have complete access to the one work we are observing.

Thus we find ourselves asking whether the infinitely intelligent infinitely creative God might create a universe like this one, and on the one hand we recognize that such a being in some sense might create anything at all; on the other hand, we find that the universe as we have it is very like something we might expect such a being to create. It has a logic of its own, inherent in its very matrix.[108] It expresses order but also chaos, grandeur but also detail, consistency but also change. Viewed as a work of art, it is remarkable on every level, and we find ourselves fascinated by everything about it, from quarks to galaxies.

The objection, then, is that it could not all have been made only for us. Yet is that a viable

---

[108] One of the foundations of western science was the belief that a rational being designed the universe and therefore the principles of its design and operation could be rationally discovered and understood. It is doubtful whether science as we know it would exist without that fundamental belief.

objection? On the one hand, we do not know that it could not have been made just for us. The fact (if it is a fact) that humanity will never visit it all, will never even understand it all in detail, hardly argues that it was not made for our sakes. We are inquisitive beings, and in this universe it is improbable that we would ever run out of that about which to inquire. As one who creates worlds for game play, I know the joy of being able to say that some of my worlds have secrets none of the players have yet discovered; if there are cave complexes under the surface of a moon orbiting a planet orbiting a star in a distant galaxy, they might well be there for us even if we never map them, there so that there is something we still do not know about the universe in which we reside.

On the other hand, we do not know that it was all made for us. God might have had many purposes for creating a universe, of which the production of humanity was only one. He tells us that the rest of the universe glorifies Him, and indeed when we consider its vastness, its order, its chaos, its beauty, and so many other attributes, it indeed causes most of us to wonder at the one who made it—at least until someone teaches us that there is no such maker, a conclusion few have reached simply from looking at it.[109] Yet it might be doing something else; other things might be happening on distant worlds. It is fun to speculate concerning what they are, but it is foolish to suppose that we know.

---

[109] It is said of Helen Keller that once communication was established with her, someone gave her the message "God, creator", and she responded, "Thank you for telling me His name." Even deaf and blind, she perceived that there was a maker of the universe.

What, though, of all the intelligent creatures populating all those galaxies, the Andorians, Bothans, Boglodites, Cardassians, Dralasites, Ewoks,[110] and the rest of the alphabet of alien races from other worlds? Do they not prove that man is an unimportant happenstance, a naturally occurring but quite ordinary exemplar of the most common sort?

As C. S. Lewis observed on this very point, in order for any condition to prove the non-existence of God, the opposite condition must be consistent with such existence, and in this case it does not work that way. If the universe proves to be teeming with intelligent life, we are told that it proves intelligence is a common result of evolution and that there is no God. On the other hand, if we are the only intelligent creatures in the universe, we are told that it proves how entirely improbable intelligence is and thus that it was a remarkable coincidence of conditions which happened against all odds to result in this unusual outcome. Yet if both conditions would disprove the existence of God, then neither really does, as either there is or is not other intelligent life in the universe, given the rules of reality, and thus if God created the universe He had to make it one way or the other, and whichever way He made it will not disprove His existence.

Yet it is noteworthy that all the above-named aliens are works of fiction, and that in one way or another they are anthropocentric designs. It is very difficult for us to design alien beings who are truly alien, a limitation of our own minds but also perhaps a limitation on what intelligence is—inquisitive,

---

[110] With apologies, in order, to *Star Trek*, *Star Wars*, *Men in Black*, again *Star Trek*, *Star Frontiers*, and again *Star Wars*.

aggressive, opportunistic, and social, these all seem to be essential qualities supporting intelligence. When we envision intelligent aliens, we make them like ourselves.[111] In essence, we make the universe a mirror of ourselves, and expect to find ourselves repeated within it, in various distortions. Telling ourselves that we are unimportant, we then make ourselves more important by modeling our imagined population of the universe after ourselves. There is at this time no reason to believe that creatures like us, nor even very intelligent creatures very different from us, exist anywhere else in the universe, other than the assumption that we are an accident likely to recur given the right conditions, and that in the vastness of accidents occurring throughout the universe some of those accidents will mirror the one that formed us. It assumes what it is trying to prove; it is a poor argument.

Some then will say it remains possible that there are such life forms out there, and we simply have not yet discovered them. Once they are discovered, we are told, that would disprove Christianity by proving that intelligent life on Earth is merely an

---

[111] Two things must be said in defense of those creating alien stories. One is that the point of most alien science fiction is not to create truly alien aliens but to create truly human aliens and use them as foils to comment on the human condition. It is because Jeriba Shigan is so human despite being alien that Willis Davidge becomes his friend in *Enemy Mine*, commenting on our attitudes to people who are different from us. The other point is that storytellers must create characters to which the listeners can relate or the story is lost. It is because we understand and reasonably fear dangerous predators like lions and bears that we are terrified by *Alien*. Truly alien creatures doing truly alien things would be interesting for exobiologists, but not so much for theatergoers.

accident. Again, it would not, for the reason already given. Further, before we could answer what the existence of other intelligent life in the universe means to Christianity, we would have to know a lot more about such intelligent life. Alien intelligent species of some types would tend to prove that Christianity is true—if, for example, they share similar beliefs in a creator and common notions of morality. It does seem to me as if Christianity at least suggests that their salvation is in some way dependent on ours, that what God did here saved the entire universe; but we do not even know that any such beings exist, nor who they are, and it would be entirely premature to be drawing any conclusions as to how that works.[112]

So, what if there are the other kinds of intelligent beings out there, the kinds that are not consistent with the Christian view of the universe?

I'm afraid that I don't know what kind that would be. Ultimately an argument based on the notion that the Christian God would not have created the universe that exists is a losing argument. There will always be things we do not understand about creation, and we will find and indeed have found facts that do not align with our limited understanding of reality, but God is too great for us

---

[112] They may already have sent their equivalent of the wise men, made aware by means unknown to us that something wonderful happened on this planet to bring redemption to the universe; and as the original wise men met the unbelieving Herod, they might meet the skeptical modern who is equally surprised to hear of the importance of that one birth. It may be, as Ray Bradbury suggested in *S Is for Space*, that Jesus ascended into the clouds as a first step to carrying His message to other planets before returning to heaven.

to be able to say what would be outside what He might create.

The Fall

There is of course an unavoidable doctrine of Christianity to the effect that God created the world good, and man brought evil and death into the world by rejecting God. To this it is answered that we now know that humanity has been on this planet a mere instant as compared against the total time of its existence, and that in that time there has been much death and decay. How can we blame man for the evil in the universe, given that it obviously predates him by at least millions of years? So much of life is based on the model of kill to eat that death could be considered one of the central aspects of life. The land masses themselves are in part formed by the deaths of millions of creatures, mostly of the plant kingdom but still deaths.

I know three plausible responses to this. Two of them I entertain as the sorts of answers that I might someday learn to be so despite my own reservations about them; the third I find sufficient. It should be understood that by "sufficient" I mean that it is an answer which causes me to recognize that there could be an answer. Being satisfied on all other points, and accepting that God is there and did in fact enter this world in the person of Jesus the Messiah, I am willing to extend a certain benefit of the doubt to Him, as it were, to accept that there will be things He has done that I will not understand fully. After all, as smart as I am, He must be smarter.

The first plausible response is that our scientific theories are all mistaken. There are some scientists who honestly believe that the universe is much younger than maintained by the majority of scientific opinion—and before you assert that they are not really scientists, remember that I in my turn had to refrain from stating that certain persons were not really Christians. They claim to be scientists; they hold advanced degrees in scientific fields and apply scientific methodologies to their studies. They might be wrong, but that does not mean they are not scientists.[113] They suggest that the strata which are supposed to demonstrate millennia of life on earth were actually created by shifting waters of a great flood. They maintain that Homo Neanderthalensis is actually Homo Sapiens Neanderthalensis—another race of the human species alongside the Mongoloid, Negroid, and Caucasoid divisions (and there are some who disagree with their model generally who at least suspect this of Neanderthal Man), and that other supposed proto-humans are either human remains or the remains of extinct hominid apes. They find problems with the evidence and evidence which appears contrary to the theories, ultimately maintaining that there could have been a six-day creation of the universe culminating in a human fall that brought death into the world.

---

[113] Some argue that these are not scientists because they do not accept the consensus of the scientific community generally. That is not a scientific attitude but a religious one. Most of those most respected in the history of science became so precisely by rejecting the general consensus in support of alternative views, and were often ridiculed for their ideas by other scientists. Even Einstein when he proposed his theory of relativity as a topic for his doctoral dissertation was met by his faculty adviser with the suggestion that he abandon this science fiction and find a more plausible subject for his thesis.

I'm afraid that my biggest problem with this answer is that my scientific education is insufficient to evaluate the data myself. Further, I suspect that everyone's scientific education is thus limited, primarily because everyone who studies science studies it in a biased environment—those who study in an environment that teaches the current preferred theories as most probably true and the creationist theories as nonsense, and those who study the evidence for the creationist theories and are taught that the modern scientific view is built on the presuppositions of atheistic naturalism. That is not to say that one side is wrong; it is to say that there is no way for the layman to know which side is right, and little way for the honest scientist himself to know whether he is on the side of truth or merely on the side he was taught to embrace.

I have a second problem, one that is connected to a point I intend to make near the end of the book, and that is that it appears that if God made the universe in six days He went to a lot of trouble to disguise the fact. Maybe He did. I'll get to that. But I cannot fault anyone for embracing the secular scientific explanation of the creation of the world. It is not that difficult to reconcile with the creation account, given that, as one ancient theologian observed, it seems to be written in the form of a folk tale—the kind of story that is intended to convey truths, not facts. Whether the six-day timetable of the first chapter of Genesis is accurate seems to me to be the least important aspect of the account.[114]

---

[114] One obstacle I faced to the day-age theory arose from the fact that water creatures and birds were said to have been created on the fifth day, land animals on the sixth. Dinosaurs seemed to belie this, as they were classed as reptiles and

My second plausible response ties into my highly metaphysical understanding of time travel theory. I have no problem with the notion that the universe existed, one way or another, and that man was created, and then at some point the fall occurred bringing the entire universe into chaos; and that because man was in some sense the lynchpin of the entire work, his fall worked backward to the dawn of time and caused all of history to be rewritten in an entirely different way, with billions of years of death and decay leading to the moment of the fall and the history of the world since then. I don't think that quite as ridiculous a notion as it sounds to most people, but I do understand why people would find it difficult.

But I have a third plausible response, which is that I'm not sure the text says what people think it says.

We are told that God created the entire universe, and that He saw that what He created was good. We are not told that there was no killing or dying, only that the totality of what was created was good. Any artist understands that dark areas are part of the beauty; any musician knows that dissonance is needed for consonance to be pleasing; any author that conflict must be present to lead to resolution. Good paintings, good symphonies, and good novels all have sections in them which convey negatives. God saw that what He made was good in its totality, and in each section of its totality.

---

predated birds.   However, more recently dinosaurs were reclassified as proto-avians, and thus are part of the creation of birds.

Man was told that he would die if he ate of the fruit of a particular tree. I don't know whether this is a literal or metaphoric tale at this point; I think it is the tale the way Adam told it to Seth. However, it does not say here that nothing else had died, only that death would come to Adam if he ate it. Nowhere in the entire Bible does it tell us that nothing had ever died before that. In fact, there is a degree to which it makes no sense for God to have told Adam he would die if nothing else had ever died—a meaningless threat.[115] Adam had to know what it meant for something to die to understand that death was something to avoid.

It also never says that man would not have died anyway. If I tell you that if you drink sulfuric acid or ethylene glycol you will die, I do not thereby mean that if you never drink those you will never die. The text in fact suggests that Adam would eventually have died, because it expresses the concern that permitted to remain in the Garden he might eat of the tree of life and live forever—and thus that he would not have lived forever before he

---

[115] There is a similar failure of reason in connection with Noah. We are told that in the Garden of Eden it never rained, but that the ground was watered by what can best be described as periodic flooding, the way the Nile watered its valley in Egypt once a year. It is then assumed that there was never any rain anywhere in the world until God ordered the flood. Yet two things tell us otherwise. The first is that when God told Noah it was going to rain, Noah already knew what that meant, and therefore rain was already part of his experience. The second is that in describing the second day of creation it is said that God created the "firmament of heaven", that is, the thing that holds the water in the sky allowing it to rain. Rain was part of the design of the world from the beginning; it just happens not to have rained in Eden.

ate of the tree of the knowledge of good and evil.
He just would not have died as soon.

Yet we know that Adam did not die on the day
that he ate the fruit; in fact, he lived quite a long
time thereafter, and had many children, according to
the accounts. In what sense did he die? The hint is
back in that Tree of Life: there was the possibility
that man might have grown to the point at which
eternal life was offered to him, but he lost that
chance when he broke the rule. So death was
always in the world, it's just that man might have
escaped it.

What of evil? Did Adam bring evil into the
world? In a sense, he probably did. He is probably
not the cause of earthquakes and floods, or of the
violence of the animal kingdom, or other natural
events which we find abhorrent; rather, he brought
something different into the world: malice.
Animals kill, but they do not kill out of hatred or
anger, only for food or self-defense.[116]   Seismic
events often kill and destroy a great number of lives,
but it is not as if the earth were trying to kill anyone.
There is no malice in those parts of creation. We
think of them as bad because we do not like the
outcomes. But then, we do not always understand
the outcomes—we still oppose forest fires, but we
have come to learn that it is our selfishness that
leads us to that opposition, that we build and we do
not want our creations destroyed by the fires, do not
want to leave the homes we have created. Fire is
part of the life cycle of the trees, of the forests, of

---

[116] Predatory animals sometimes play with prey creatures. This
is particularly noticed among felines. While the way a cat
corners a mouse and seemingly taunts it before killing it seems
cruel to us, for the cat it is practice, honing its hunting skills.

the atmosphere, of the earth itself. It is on some level good when an old growth forest burns, allowing new growth to emerge from the newly fertilized soil. We are confusing that which inconveniences and displeases us with that which is malevolent or malicious. Nature has a lot of death and rebirth—part of the pattern God wanted to teach in anticipation of the resurrection of Christ—but it has no malicious intent, no real evil, just a lot of violent change we would prefer did not occur.

Is this a credible understanding of the passage? I think it is, based on a few observations about it. We are told that when Adam and Eve ate the fruit of the Tree of the Knowledge of Good and Evil, their eyes were in some sense opened, and they saw that they were naked, and they clothed themselves; but despite having clothed themselves they were still afraid when God returned to the garden, so they hid themselves. Now, it certainly was not wrong for them to be naked; God had made them naked, and saw that it was good. It also was not wrong for them to be clothed, because at the end of the story God made clothes for them, and He would not have done so had wearing clothes been wrong. So what is the point of the clothes? The point, which we miss because clothes are so basic a part of our lives, is that clothes protect you. To be naked is to be vulnerable. Adam and Eve were always vulnerable before the fall, but were unaware of their vulnerability until suddenly, having somehow gotten knowledge, each of them became aware that there were things he or she could do to the other that would be malicious and harmful, and conversely that the other could do such hurtful things to him or her. Clothes were needed to protect them from each other. But clothes could not protect them from God —He was ultimately too dangerous, and even though He had never indicated in any way that He might hurt them, He could hurt them, and they lost their trust in Him and hid.

Thus what they gained was the ability to be malicious, to be wicked or evil toward others, and the corresponding fear that others would be malicious toward them. That malice became part of the projected expectations—we came to think that lions, wolves, and other predators liked to kill for the thrill of it, instead of that they hunted for food; we envisioned malicious spirits and gods, and when we moved beyond these we shifted to malicious aliens. It perhaps drove us into tribes for mutual protection, but it also isolated us from each other by our own paranoia.

It did not have to happen before the dawn of human history, because there was no malice or wickedness of that sort in the world, there was only natural death and predatory feeding which is not malicious, not evil, only something we find distasteful—and, worth noting, we can only claim is evil if we accept that good and evil exist as realities above the material world.

What about the trappings, the Garden and the Trees and the Serpent? I don't know; I was not there. Maybe the story is entirely literal, and the first truly human creatures existed in some sort of extra-dimensional space created just for them (the description of the rivers is counter-intuitive, as they begin together and flow away from each other) until they were exiled. Maybe it is entirely metaphorical, that the story was the best way the truth could be preserved and conveyed to the next generation. I don't think that the truths it conveys about us should be discounted simply because we're not certain of the facts.

An aside on that subject, someone is bound to mention that Adam is the first of a long list of impossibly long-lived people, ranging from two hundred to nearly a thousand years. The average age of the first twelve people given in the line of descent from Seth is eight hundred one years. That use to bother me. I was unhappy with the most common explanation, that these are dynasties, because it doesn't explain the dates of the births of the sons. Then I was reading some material on gerontology,[117] and came upon the discovery of a simple code in our genome, involving three genes, which triggers a biological self-destruct mechanism by which our bodies degenerate significantly very quickly. The author, not at all interested in biblical genealogies, asserted that if we could deactivate that code the average lifespan of humans would be about eight hundred years. It thus is within the realm of possibility that the earliest humans lived that long, and that at some point this limiting mutation was activated. It is of course contrary to standard evolutionary hypotheses, because the same system is undoubtedly found in other primates; but we cannot know that it is not so.

But quite apart from that possible explanation, there is nothing essential to the Christian faith in the recorded ages of the ancients; it could simply be information we do not at this point understand.

---

[117] This was in Omni magazine; I have lost my collection and do not know the issue or the title or author of the article.

Hell

At one time, the notion that those who do not believe would be sent to hell as punishment was put forward as an argument in favor of faith; today it is raised as an objection. The objection is, if God is the loving God as Christians claim, why would He send people into a horrible eternal punishment simply for not embracing certain beliefs about Him during a brief human lifespan? Yet this objection is fraught with misunderstandings at just about every turn, from where such people are going to why they are going there.

The word hell itself is an old English word that originally represented the place of the dead generally; it only later took the meaning of the place of punishment, and much of our imagery of hell comes not from the Bible but from medieval conceptions of a place of punishment. In the Old Testament, it speaks much of a place called "Sheol", a place of the dead roughly equivalent to the grave but suggesting some form of continuation after death. The New Testament mostly uses the word "Hades",[118] originally the equivalent of "Hades'" that is, "Hades' home", again the place (in Greek mythology) where the dead go. In one place it mentions "Tartarus"[119] as a place where rebellious angels were sent. Jesus spoke primarily of "Gehenna",[120] to which we will return in a moment.

There is mention, in Revelation, of a lake of fire. Revelation, though, is apocalyptic—which means that it is filled with metaphoric imagery conveying

---

[118] E.g., Matthew 11:23, Acts 2:31, Revelation 1:18.
[119] II Peter 2:4.
[120] E.g., Matthew 5:22.

ideas through pictures. It is given as the ultimate doom of the devil, and of death itself. What it means, though, is unclear precisely because it is a metaphor, and we do not know for what it stands.

That also becomes a problem, although a lesser problem, with "Gehenna". In this case, the problem is that we have lost the metaphor. "Gehenna" literally means "Valley of Hinnom", a place just outside Jerusalem which had gone from an ancient place of pagan worship and sacrifice to a then-modern landfill, the place where all of the city dumped its garbage for centuries. It is a place of which Jesus says "the worm never dies and the fires never extinguish", because that is a description of such a collection of trash and garbage, as it composts, decomposes, and spontaneously combusts. The threat that this contains is one of being tossed in the trash. The images of eternal torture are not found in the Bible, except by extrapolation from these metaphors. Jesus also spoke of being shut out in the outer darkness, another metaphor for this punishment, in this case about being excluded from whatever good things are happening somewhere else. Like many ancient teachers, Jesus taught with hyperbole, using extremes to emphasize differences. It is the matter of saying that A is so good, missing A would be as bad as B, which is clearly terrible. If you miss heaven, by contrast it is like being consigned to the garbage dump. We do not know exactly what heaven and hell are like, but we know that it is something like the contrast between living in an eternal wedding feast and living in an eternal lake of fire. You really want the one and you really want to avoid the other, but both are metaphors for the real thing, which we cannot describe or understand from our present perspective.

The objection will be raised that this is still "punishment", and it is cruel of God to "punish" people for a few small mistakes in life. The better word, though, is "retribution", and it is a better word because it means being repaid for the harm you caused others. Each of us has harmed someone at some time, and we owe a debt because of it, a repayment we should make. It is an obligation easily overlooked, but more easily seen when we reverse it: all of us have said of someone, "He owes me." We have been harmed by someone, and we believe (correctly, as it turns out) that it is only fair that that person compensate us for the harm he did to us, and that he lose any benefit he gained from harming us. Yet we are equally to blame in the eyes of someone else, for whom we are the person who ought to compensate for the wrong done.

We might claim that it was not our fault, that we were forced into that position by someone else. The thief claims that if it were not for the cruelty of others toward him he would not have had to steal to meet the needs of his family. Those others are guilty of what they did to him, and to the degree that he is right about their responsibility for his subsequent actions, they are guilty for this, too. Yet that does not make him innocent. So, too, you may have felt forced to do wrong because others had done wrong to you, and they are guilty of your wrongs, and you are guilty of your wrongs, and as perhaps inevitably happens when the one you wronged wrongs someone else, you share that guilt as well. If there is justice, we are all guilty, owing debts beyond what we can afford.

Christianity says that God has offered a deal: give up all your claims against anyone and everyone else, and God will free you of all your debts to anyone and everyone else, making payment on your behalf where necessary.

It is complicated at this point. The argument is that to get this deal you have to believe certain claimed doctrines, and there is a sense in which that is obviously true, and another sense in which it is arrant nonsense. God is not interested in whether you embrace theological constructs of the trinity, the dual nature of Christ, the expiatory effects of sacrifice, the power of some ritual. He is interested in whether you trust Him. That is what faith in God means: that you trust God. Of course, to trust God you have to believe that there is a god, and that He is that God. You might trust the spirit of a mountain, or an ancient tree, or a planet or star, but these are not The God Who makes this offer. The question then becomes whether you agree to trust God to forgive your debts on the terms He offers, or decide to pay them all yourself and stay away from God. The "theology" is a matter of whether you trust the right God, that is, whether you are trusting the God who actually made the offer, instead of inventing some other god in whom to place your trust. You do not need to fully comprehend Who God is to trust Him, but it is important that you are trusting Him, not some other god.

At this point it is again all metaphor, on some level. Yet we can use metaphor to grasp what we cannot see directly. Imagine that you are outside in a strange world in the evening, and there is one building with one door. Standing in the door is a fierce creature—perhaps a lion, perhaps a dragon. He calls to you, tells you that night is coming and all who are outside will freeze, but you are welcome to come inside and keep warm by his fire before he bars the door against the cold for the night. You then must choose. Either you must trust the lion, the dragon, and enter his home, or you must instead decide that the risk is great that he might eat you, that he must have an ulterior motive for offering you this option, and that he is misleading you concerning the dangers of the night, that you will be able to survive it. If you do not choose to enter, you by default choose to remain outside. This is the choice you face. God does not send anyone to hell; He invites people to escape hell and come with Him to heaven.

It is always more complicated than the metaphor, which is why there are so many metaphors. The price of admittance is a surrendering of your own rights and claims against others (there will be no fighting or resentments allowed within those walls). You cannot see the house, and perhaps you cannot see the lion, when you make the decision—you receive a notice, a proclamation sent out to the world, not even necessarily to you personally although made personal in its invitation. The question almost becomes whether you will trust the lion who might not exist based on the contents of the letter. Perhaps there is no coming night, no warm home, nothing to fear. The invitation could be a sham; worse, it could be a lure. Yet if it is a lure, then there is not nothing beyond death, and it might be important to learn what.[121]

---

[121] Prior to writing this book, I had written an answer, using a different metaphor, to the problem specifically of God "sending" people to hell. The short version is that God "sends" no one to hell, but everyone is headed there, and God offers a way of escape. The slightly longer version appears at the end of this book, as "Appendix: Sent to Hell?".

Monotheism

To this point the discussion has been focused on addressing the question of whether there is any god at all. Yet there is an opposite pole to this, the question of why I believe there is only one God, and why I particularly think it is this one.

There is a sense in which the answer might reasonably be stated as "I don't", that is, I do not believe necessarily that there is only one god. After all, language is mutable. On one level, Humpty Dumpty is right: words mean what the user wants them to mean, no more and no less.[122] To my dog, perhaps I am a god; I provide his food and drink, keep him sheltered, and magically open the portals that allow him to enter and leave. Meanwhile, dogs (not mine, but working dogs) are god-like to sheep, keeping them safe and directing their paths. We use the word in ways that do not necessarily indicate the one almighty source of all being.

We can accept, as well, that if there is a god there is probably also a world of spirits. Judaism accepted as much, speaking of spirit messengers appearing to and conversing with people God had selected, and occasionally suggesting that there were also spirits opposed to us, possibly to God. In one of the oldest stories in the Bible, the Book of Job,[123] we are introduced to a spirit who is against us, and

---

[122] This from Lewis Carroll's *Through the Looking Glass and What Alice Found There*, in which the heroine has an extended discussion with the egg sitting on the wall, and Carroll plays several games with words and our perceptions of reality. Humpty Dumpty uses a word in a way Alice does not understand, so he explains what he means by it, and she objects that the word does not mean that—to which the egg offers that reply.

the later book of Daniel includes mention of a messenger spirit being opposed by some other spirit who did not want the message delivered. God is not the only spirit, and never claimed to be.

Furthermore, Israel always recognized that other nations had gods, and never questioned whether those gods had any reality. When in I Samuel 5 the Philistine idol Dagon was reported to have fallen on its face before the captured Ark of the Covenant (the seat of God on Earth), the obvious implication is that the engraved statue was a surrogate for a real spirit being, a real god of some kind, who did real wonders on behalf of his own people the Philistines. Israel were not exactly monotheists; they were henotheists, people who believed that there were other gods but that they were to serve only this one, who was the God of gods, the greatest of all the gods.[124] He also claims to have been the creator of

---

[123] It is difficult to date the contents of this book. The writing is characteristic of the period in which other wisdom literature, such as Proverbs and Ecclesiastes, was composed, but the story recounts details of a much earlier time in the land from which Abraham emigrated.

[124] Recently some archaeologists asserted that having found household idols in pre-captivity Israeli homes they proved that Israel was not devoted to one God prior to that captivity, as if it were a later invention. This confuses the official religion of Judaism of the time with the practices of the Jewish people in the land, and ignores the plain testimony of the biblical historic texts. The prophets and other writers made it quite plain that among the people idolatry was widely practiced, and that the one God of Israel who had brought them into the land was greatly displeased and was going to change things. The point is made that the captivity itself was not the result of greater military might defeating a small nation, but of God deciding that His people were to be punished for their infidelity to Him. The religion of Jeremiah, of Isaiah, of Elijah, of David, of Gideon, of Abraham, of Noah, and of all the key persons

all, and presumably of all the other spirit beings who take the title "god" for themselves.

So let us assume that there are other "gods" out there. The real question at that point is not whether you believe that they exist, but which ones can you trust? One has given us a long history of His relationships with people, beginning with the line of people represented as the heirs of Adam, culminating in His demonstration that He loves us enough to be willing to die for us.[125] It could be a massive con, some attempt to fool as many humans as possible into trusting this one spirit, this one divine imposter. On the other hand, when it comes to demonstration of trustworthiness, there is no divinity with better credentials than this one.

And ultimately, as concerns any and all other deities, we do not know. If there is a Dagon, an Odin, a Zeus, if the gods of the far east or the near east or the Americas or Africa or any others are real spirits, real gods, can we trust them, can we know that they are not the ones running the con, trying to lure people into some trap for purposes which make sense in the spirit realm which we could not comprehend? They may seem nice enough, as Doctor Who once said of a thief of whom Romana

---

between and before was a declaration of fidelity to this one God, frequently with a condemnation of those often many Israelites who worshipped other gods.

[125] It is also significant that most of what this God has revealed is connected to history, as events in the lives of people and nations, rather than in the main as myths. Although some assert Old Testament accounts to be myths, this is based primarily on the conclusion that the miracles reported did not occur, which is circular reasoning. The events are placed in a framework of history, in real places connected to real people, once we have left the Garden of Eden behind.

claimed he had an honest face, "Well, he wouldn't make a very good thief with a *dis*honest face, now, would he?"[126] If a spirit is trying to con us, we are not very well equipped to know it. We might think we are in control, but there is no way to know that it is not just some elaborate plan to claim us for themselves.

That is, of course, true of Christianity, that The God we worship might be leading us into a trap. Yet on the one hand, He has done everything possible to assure us otherwise, and on the other hand, if He is, what other hope do we have that is more assured? Returning to our metaphor of the lion (or dragon) in the doorway, our landscape changes to include a world filled with other creatures, each of which is inviting us into its own unseen home, and we face the decision not only of whether we can trust the lion, but whether we can trust the tiger, the bear, the wolf, any of the others who beckon for us to follow them somewhere else. If the lion has already introduced himself to us and showed that we can trust him, he becomes the obvious choice.

As a footnote to this, there are some who claim that many of the stories of the Bible are derived from older stories. There is a Babylonian creation story with some elements similar to those of Genesis; there are stories of floods destroying the world and a man building a great ship to save the animals. The problem with such claims is that they assume the Biblical accounts are the later and therefore derivative stories. The Biblical accounts

---

[126] Doctor Who, *The Ribos Operation*, first in *The Key to Time* series, starring Tom Baker and produced by the British Broadcasting Company (BBC).

are generally the simpler, less fanciful versions. Is it really more likely that a writer would create a simplified version of a familiar tale than that he would take a simpler familiar tale and elaborate on it? A late date for the Genesis accounts was built on the same sort of scholarship that suggested late dates for the Gospels (which we have already seen are untenable), relying on the notion that the stories could not be true and therefore could not have been contemporary. Yet even if we do not accept the notion that written records were passed down to Joseph, stored in the libraries of Egypt, and accessed by Moses, it is still entirely possible that rather than being dependent on each other both are dependent on the same earlier written versions, or on oral traditions from the same actual events. (Whether we believe there was a world-wide flood or merely a regional disaster is a separate question, and beyond the scope of the present consideration.) Similarities between the Biblical accounts and the tales of other ancient religions could well suggest both rely on the same earlier sources.

Personal

If you ask Christians why they are so certain of their belief in God, you will inevitably come to the point at which they leave logic behind and tell you they just know. At that point, those looking for proof throw up their hands and declare that it is illogical, that that is not evidence. Yet it is evidence, and evidence of the most common sort. The Christian message in the first century was proclaimed by people who claimed that they had met the risen Christ. Their "proof" was not that it was logical or inevitable that they would have done so, but simply that they were witnesses. In much the same way, Christians today—myself included—are declaring that God is real and Christ is alive not primarily because it's logical or there's a strong historic foundation for it, but because we, too, have met Him. We have not met Jesus in His physical resurrected body here on earth, because a short while after His resurrection He was seen to leave this world and vanish into the clouds, claiming He was going to wait for us in heaven.[127] Yet we have

---

[127] Appearances thereafter were mostly visions, but there is the one case of the Apostle Paul. He claims to have seen Jesus in bodily form after the resurrection, while he was traveling to Damascus in Acts 9. This is the only recorded bodily appearance after the Ascension. However, in Corinthians Paul suggests that this meeting was reversed, that Jesus did not return to earth but snatched Paul to heaven for a few minutes. Noteworthy, too, in this event is that Paul was so far from believing the resurrection of Jesus that he was arresting Christians for preaching what he regarded a dangerous heretical lie; it was this encounter with Jesus that changed his view and caused him to become the famed Christian missionary of history.

met Him, and known Him to be a real person involved in our lives.

Saint Augustine is translated as having said, "You have made us for yourselves, and our hearts are restless until they find their rest in You." It is said by some that we all are seeking something we cannot quite identify, and satisfaction remains elusive; yet there is an argument that if we have a desire, there must exist a satisfaction—thirst is satisfied by water, hunger by food, curiosity by information. Some who then have embraced faith in God claim that they found what they were always seeking; they further claim that the desire for that which is satisfied by finding God proves that God exists.

In connection with this, there have been researches recently that suggest an altered mental state associated with meditation and spiritual communion. Some argue from this that the existence of such a mental state demonstrates that man was designed for some sort of spiritual communion, and thus that the spiritual world must be real, something we are in essence programmed to desire and seek.

It is objected by some that they are not seeking any such thing, that they have no desire to discover God. It is relevant to this that some who have embraced faith have said that they never realized they were seeking this until they were confronted by it and embraced it; it thus makes sense that there would be those who do not recognize the desire within themselves. It is also relevant that many of those who do not recognize any desire for God frequently exhibit a hunger for something else— scientific knowledge, romantic love, perfect sex—

and that these objects remain either elusive or dissatisfying. If that desire were for such things, we would expect that it would be satisfied upon attaining them, and that they would indeed be attainable.

It is also objected that the desire itself does not prove the existence of the object desired. Many desire the perfect mate, and despite claims by some that they have found just that person most of us recognize that every person and every relationship has flaws. The perfect book has not been written, nor the perfect music composed, nor the perfect picture painted, despite our desires to find these ideals. Yet some find satisfaction for their desires in a mate who is right for them, or in artistic creations which approach perfection. Hunger can be satisfied; thirst can be quenched.

Many claim that the desire for that elusive object they could never quite define was satisfied in God. It may be that the existence of the desire does not prove the existence of the desired; it may be that the satisfaction of the desire does not prove the existence of the satisfier. However, the testimony of people to the effect that in God they found what they had always been seeking, whether knowingly or ignorantly, is at least suggestive that such a God exists and can be known.

I was headlining (with The Last Psalm) at an evangelistic concert at Farleigh Dickenson University, and sitting in the back by the book table while someone else was performing, when a student noticed me and engaged me in discussion. He said that there were so many people there who somehow thought they could know what he and I (including me as a person of obvious intellect) knew you could not know. I objected: I know. How could I know, he asked? Yet it is not that difficult. We can perhaps easily imagine how in the ancient world reports of sights from distant lands would be carried by word of mouth or in written texts, and people would be doubtful. Whether it was the description of an elephant, or of the Sphinx in Egypt, or of the geysers of Yellowstone, there is an aspect of the report that relies on the credibility of witnesses delivering what seems an incredible account.[128] Yet those able to see an elephant, or the Sphinx, or the geysers, have no doubts of their existence, and become the witnesses who attest to their reality. We earlier addressed the issues related to eyewitness testimony, but the best evidence for the existence of a person you have never met is the testimony of someone you trust that such a person exists—and the claim that such a person does not exist requires a significantly higher level of proof in the face of such testimony. In the same way, Christians are people

---

[128] There is a tale of an early American explorer who appeared in a town on the eastern bank of the Mississippi claiming to have been on its western side, to have spent weeks wandering lost, to have escaped Indians and struggled to return to civilization, because he knew he had to tell someone what he had discovered. Then as he began to describe some of what he had seen at what is now Yellowstone National Park his previously eager audience decided that his entire story was fiction, because such things as he now described could not exist. It is natural to weigh the credibility of the witness against the credibility of the account, but incredible accounts reported by incredible witnesses are sometimes true, and an incredible account from a credible witness should be given more credibility. That there might be a spirit world is certainly something the reader has a right to doubt, but claiming that a witness known otherwise to be sane and honest who reports having encountered something from such a world is mistaken or lying is a rather serious accusation.

who have met Christ, have met God, and so know that He is real not because it is logical but because of an actual encounter.

At this point many are about to toss the book aside. You wanted proof that you could see, and you cannot actually see Jesus being involved in my life. That is why I began with everything else—the intellectual proofs, the discussion of what evidence there is that God exists and that Jesus is God, the reasons the objections are not fatal to that—and only now come to this. It cannot be proven by words in a book that I have met Jesus, any more than it can be proven by words in a book that I have met Barry McGuire[129] or John McLaughlin,[130] or that I married Janet Brown, or that I am the father of Ryan

---

[129] Thrice, actually—once at a concert he did in or about 1976 in or near Boston, Massachusetts, once when I opened for him at the Gordon College March Thaw in 1977, and once when I interviewed him live at the studios of WNNN-FM in or about 1983. Barry McGuire was a member of the music group The New Christie Minstrels, star of the musical *Hair* on Broadway, and by the early 1970s a leading figure in the contemporary Christian music field.

[130] That is, the guitarist. In 1974 I worked backstage security for his concert with the Mahavishnu Orchestra at Fairleigh Dickenson University; I learned the trick to playing harmonics leads from watching him practice before the show, although I have never mastered it.

Young.[131] You can trust my word about it, or you can tell me that I am deceived or lying.

However, I can tell you more than that I have met Him and have an ongoing relationship, because I can tell you about that relationship.

---

[131] I could produce documentary evidence of the latter two claims, but these are still words on pages and do not prove what they assert of my relationships. They are ultimately simply written versions of the testimony of witnesses. It might be asserted that DNA evidence can prove my parentage of Ryan Young (on the assumption that I have neither an identical twin nor a clone), and by means of that some form of relationship to his mother Janet, but while we think that is scientific evidence, here in the book it would again be merely the testimony of witnesses—in this case, of the people who took the DNA samples and ran the comparisons.

Guidance

When I was a senior in high school, I had a very sketchy notion about my future. Spring had arrived, and I had not as much as named a college in which I might be interested. Of course, my plans at the time were to become a Christian rock musician (never mind that at the time these were few and far between, there were some records so someone was making a living at it) and that was not something for which an educational path was obvious. My parents, however, informed me that in the fall I would either be in school somewhere or have a job —and what kind of job does one get with a college prep high school diploma? So I prayed about it honestly, telling God that I would do whatever he directed, but I did not feel ready to enter the work world. Then, for some strange reason, I stopped thinking about it.

I attended a weekly Bible study connected to an ecumenical youth group in which that Presbyterian church I mentioned not joining was a participant. It happened that my then long-time sound technician and more recent bass guitarist was also in that group, and his Lutheran parents (whose church also participated) hosted and led this Bible study in their home. That week as the session opened, they announced that having finished what they had planned to cover ahead of schedule, they had invited a friend who was a student at a nearby Lutheran Bible college to share some of what he had learned about one of the most challenging books in the Bible, Revelation.[132] I was not fascinated by his

---

[132] In Catholic Bibles entitled Apocalypse. The words are nearly synonymous, "revelation" coming from the Latin for

presentation, but was captivated by the information that there was a Bible college nearby. It would mean I could attend a school (thus satisfying my parents) while learning more about the Bible (thus better preparing myself for my envisioned future as a Christian musician) and staying close to home (continuing to work with the band). I secured information about the college, and told my mother I was interested in investigating it.

We—my mother and I—visited the small campus about twenty miles away; we happened to meet both the President of the College and the head of the Bible Studies department, and had good talks with both of them. I very much liked what I saw, and applied immediately.

That weekend I had practice with the band's lead guitarist, my best friend and the only other member of the band graduating high school that year. I knew he might be leaving, but I hadn't thought that far ahead. He asked me what my plans were for next year, and I replied, "I've applied to Luther College;" he looked at me so strangely, I thought I should add, "in Teaneck," which only made his look the stranger. Had he heard of it? In fact, he had been accepted there and would be attending in the fall. Not only was I not losing my lead guitar player, he was headed for the same Bible college where we would see a lot more of each other.[133]

"unveiling" and "apocalypse" coming from the Greek for "uncovering".

[133] He actually lived a few miles from the school, and so it was a bit of a commute for him to come to practices and we had rarely spent much time together outside that. Perhaps his proximity to the school makes it more likely that he would also attend there, but he was not Lutheran, either (he was Presbyterian), and the school was tiny, with fewer than two

I was recounting all of this to that bass guitarist at whose home it all started one afternoon after school, and decided, aloud, that if I were accepted there I would conclude that this was where the Lord wanted me to go.

My acceptance letter was awaiting me when I got home that day. My mother immediately called the school and got the head of the department on the phone, who was surprised that a decision had been made so quickly. I never had any doubt as to whether God wanted me there; He had made it clear enough for me.

My attendance at Luther College was in many ways pivotal in my life. The band picked up a drummer who made a significant difference, and together we became about as successful as a local Christian rock band could be at that time. I learned a great deal about the Bible, and about thinking about all of life from the focus of what I believe rather than compartmentalizing "religion" into one part of life. I also met my wife, whom I married a year and a half after graduation. There is no question that much of the course of my life since then sprang from that time.

You can certainly write it off as coincidence, and say I am irrationally reading purpose into a random chain of events, and I cannot prove you wrong. I can, however, recount similar stories in connection with my later attendance at Gordon College and at Widener University School of Law, my position at WNNN-FM, my appointment as Chaplain of the Christian Gamers Guild, my involvement in writing Multiverser and several of the other books I have

---

hundred students enrolled in all programs.

written, my marriage, my membership in the
Seventh-Day Baptist Church of Shiloh, the forming
of several of the bands in which I played or which I
directed, finding the homes in which we have lived,
the cars we've owned, some of the conventions I've
attended, and much more. These combinations of
circumstances and prompting are one of the ways
God most often directs me, and I recognize them as
from Him. He does not generally speak to me from
a burning bush or a flaming mountain; He already
did that for someone else, and the infinitely creative
Creator does not really like to repeat Himself. I am
persuaded, though, that He is directing me.

Protection

There was a storm when I was at college, and a tall tree in my parents' back yard was struck by lightning, the top of it coming down onto the lawn and driveway. Nothing was damaged and no one was hurt, but there was a significant amount of cleanup to do, and I came home that weekend to help my father and brother work on it. We had all been Boy Scouts and Scout leaders, and so had ample training in woodcraft and safety, and had an axe, a handsaw, and a chain saw between us. The heavy sections had to be cut into fireplace-sized pieces and stacked to dry, the scrap and leaves hauled into the woods to compost, and we were working on it for a few hours.

There came a moment when my brother, working with the chain saw, upended a heavy limb to flip it over the fallen trunk for a better angle at cutting it. As the far end came down it headed straight for me—which I did not see until it hit me, and no one else saw soon enough to as much as shout. We had no hardhats; it could have split my head open, or broken my shoulder or my spine. It was potentially a very serious accident.

As it happened, I was fine. I had an instant before been undecided what to do next and started up the hill, then changed my mind and reversed direction, and so was moving at the instant the branch came down. At the other end, the heavy bottom of the branch had dug into the dirt beside the trunk, and so the base had stopped moving; the top had momentum and continued downward, but was already losing force against its own spring. When it reached me, it tapped me on the shoulder and pulled back, brushing my face in the most minor of ways. I was startled, stunned a bit from how close it was, but in essence unharmed and unhurt.

Mendelssohn wrote a chorus as part of *The Elijah* which I had sung in several choirs, a setting of the words, "For He has given His angels a charge concerning thee, that they keep thee safely and guard thee in thy ways."[134] That music immediately was playing in my head, as I saw God's protective hand preventing a serious accident.

You would be wrong to say that no accident happened; a very serious accident happened. My father, who since spent many years working with the volunteer ambulance service, often quipped, "Don't be there when the accident happens." The accident happened; the tree branch made an uncontrolled fall that would have cracked my skull had I been three inches farther up the hill, or broken my shoulder or spine if it had kept its momentum for another few inches. I was not there; I had moved—or perhaps been moved—out of the path, and the branch had stopped—or perhaps been stopped—before it reached me.

I have been in multiple automotive accidents. In some of them my car was totaled; in some someone else's car was totaled, while mine took minimal damage; in some cars brushed each other at high speed and took surprisingly little damage. In all of them, I walked away unscathed. Some will say that it is a testament to the effectiveness of seat belts and the good training my father provided in reinforcing the necessity of wearing them whenever you are in a moving vehicle. That is certainly part of it. Yet with every accident and every close call (I do an

---

[134] This is a setting of Psalm 91:11.

above average amount of driving) I see again God's protective hand.

Prayer

I am not what they call a "prayer warrior". I pray, and I believe that God is hearing me and acting in accordance with my prayers. However, I have seen few enough specific answers to specific requests that I tend to avoid making them, and when people ask me to pray for them I always agree to do so but sometimes suggest that they might do better to ask someone else. Someone has said that God always answers prayers, but sometimes the answer is "No".[135] I'm not certain of the theology of that, but that seems to be the answer I most commonly get.

However, I believe in the power of prayer, and I have seen it. Some people, even some members of my family, get prayers answered reliably and swiftly. That does not mean *always* or *immediately*; nor should we expect that. Yet the car for which my wife prayed, which she got for less than half its book value when all indications were that it was worth more than book value, is just one small evidence that God is listening and answering. She spends time every day thanking God for His goodness to her, surprised that He treats her so well.

Objectors will say that you cannot prove the power of prayer, that nearly all prayers can be explained otherwise. Pray for healing, but there is evidence that positive thinking is itself powerful medicine. Pray for the weather you need, whether rain for the crops or sunshine for the harvest festival, but weather is already terribly unpredictable and you might get what you want without asking. Some

---

[135] The statement also says that sometimes the answer is "Wait".

answers could be coincidental; some could be caused by the acts of the one praying. No one I know gets everything he requests, and those who get answers most consistently tend to be thoughtful concerning what they ask. George Müller always prayed for the needs of his orphanages and never spoke of them before they were met, and while help did not always arrive the day he prayed it always arrived before the need was critical, and he supported thousands of orphans without ever holding a fundraiser or asking anyone other than God for a penny. Certainly eventually people were aware that he ran orphanages and would need support, but it did not begin that way. His is one of the more dramatic accounts, but there are many others, men and women whose lives and ministries were supported entirely by prayer. It is obvious that God answers prayers.

Why, though, can it not be proved? That means, really, why can we not experiment on God. We generally do not like it when others experiment on us, attempting to manipulate us. Why should we expect God to cooperate with an experiment? Arguably, too, He has already cooperated with human efforts to test whether He hears and answers prayers, and we can read much of that in the Bible. Certainly in the realm of the hard sciences replication is an important aspect of experimentation; but when we are talking about trying to prove that someone is there, the fact that this is a person means that He may well respond differently to the same repeated effort. You cannot prove God answers prayer for the same reason that you cannot prove I have a weakness for chocolate: He will not necessarily respond the same way every time, because every time is different if only by virtue of the fact that it has been done before.

It is of course still more complicated than that. There is the problem that people are often asking opposing requests. The picnickers pray for fair weather for their outing while the farmer is begging for rain for the crops, and although sometimes God manages both, that is a difficult trick meteorologically, and it is more likely that He will answer one prayer or the other. (A little rain is not satisfactory to either supplicant in this case.) There are undoubtedly thousands of people praying to win the lottery, but they cannot all win.

It is still more complicated than that, too. Let us suppose that someone comes to my office door and asks me for twenty dollars. If it is my wife, I will dig into my pocket and see whether I have twenty dollars; I might mention to her that I had intended to use it for something else, but she certainly can have it if she still wants it. My readiness to part with the cash, though, decreases in accordance with who is asking—one of my sons, one of our extended houseguests, a visitor. In all such cases I will almost certainly ask why they need or want the money; I am more likely to give my (grown) kids money for gasoline or pizza than for cigarettes or beer. I may also take into account that person's circumstances and the nature of the request—someone asking to borrow twenty dollars until he is paid at the end of the week is more likely to get the money than someone who hopes to get it for nothing; the son who agrees to mow the lawn or who has just washed the dishes is more likely to get it than one who has been playing video games all week; indeed, if giving someone twenty dollars saves me from having to make dinner tonight, that might well be reason to agree. I don't always give money to those who ask, and I don't always refuse, and sometimes I don't state my reasons.

Further, sometimes people pray for what is not really best for themselves or for others. We have an example of this in the ministry of Isaiah,[136] in which he announced to the relatively good King Hezekiah of Judah that his current sickness would be the end of his life, and when Hezekiah prayed to God that it might not be so God changed his mind, allowing him to live another score of years. However, in that time Hezekiah fathered a boy named Manasseh, who became one of the worst kings Judah ever had—a king who would never have been born had Hezekiah not persuaded God to allow him to live a little longer. Someone has spoken of those petitions which heaven in mercy declines to grant, and we have probably all prayed them.[137]

We have also prayed prayers which prove selfish even when they appear otherwise. Many will pray that a loved one not die, not because the loved one would be happier alive but because the one praying would be saddened by the loss. Paul's comments in the first chapter of his letter to the Philippians suggest that for the believer, our time on earth is something of a burden to be borne as long as we are needed here, and death the doorway to the better world when we can retire.[138] We mourn our dead as

---

[136] II Kings 20.

[137] This is probably a misremembering of Hannah More's *Moses in the Bulrushes, Part I*, which reads in part, "So ignorant and blind, that did not God/Sometimes withhold in mercy what we ask,/We should be ruined at our own request."

[138] Philippians 1:21ff. It should be recognized that Paul is writing from prison and faces the possibility of execution, and

they themselves rejoice—which is not to say we ought not mourn for our own loss, but that we should recognize that death is not sad for the one who by it enters the presence of God, only for those of us who must wait to see him again in what for us is the passage of a long stretch of years but from the perspective of eternity a mere blink of an eye.[139]

Yet why does God, Who claims to be fully impartial in His judgments, grant the prayers of some and not of others? Perhaps more specifically, why should He not grant my petitions?

Just as those who ask me for money do not know my reasons for giving or refusing, I do not know why God tends not to answer my prayers. I do know, though, some possible reasons that are not true.

The first is that the fact He does not often answer my prayers does not mean he does not answer prayers generally. That I might give twenty dollars to one son and not to another does not mean I never give money when asked; it only means that I am selective in my giving. That God chooses not to grant my requests does not mean He does not grant

---

thus he is speaking of his own possible death (not callously suggesting that it is better that someone else died). He suggests that death is the better outcome for himself, but that his readers still need him alive so he anticipates being released from his imprisonment.

[139] Some will object that we do not know our loved ones are in a better place. Yet if we would believe, or even suppose, that there is a God willing to hear and answer our prayers, should we not also accept what He claims is our eternal destiny? There is an objection that we do not know with any certainty which of our family members have embraced God's offered mercy and which have rejected it, but then our prayers should certainly be not that they would live but that they would turn to God before they died.

requests; it means that for some reason He decided it would be better not to grant mine.

Nor does it mean God is not impartial, nor that He does not love or have concern for me. Impartiality does not mean that we all get identical benefits—food stamps are not issued to millionaires, those who are healthy are not given free beds in hospitals, and no one is permitted to call himself "surgeon" without graduating from medical school. The claim that all men are created equal is what is called a legal fiction. No one really believes that Elvis and Einstein would have been interchangeable, however much we respect their respective gifts. That God treats all of us equally means on some level that He treats each of us differently. God has treated me well in many ways—not the least of which is the intelligence He gave me, which enables me to understand much about Him and about so much else.

Were I to enumerate other gifts God has given me, it might begin to sound as if I could do everything and had no need of anyone. That is not so, and I am keenly aware of several of my shortcomings. Yet it underscores another reason. God intended for us to be mutually dependent, to need each other and to serve each other. It may be that were God as free with answers to my prayers as He is with some others, I would not recognize that I need people almost as much as I need God.

There are several other points to consider in this regard. Why do I want God to answer my prayers? Is it because I am testing whether He cares for me, despite all He has done to demonstrate this otherwise? Is it because I am looking for easy solutions to difficult situations? Is it because I don't like what He has chosen for my life and think I can run my own life better if He will just cooperate with my plans? Those are all good reasons for God not to give what I request. At the same time, why does God not simply give me what I ask? Is it because He wants me to find the solutions to my problems, because He is trying to teach me something, or improve my character, or build my confidence? Is it because I am requesting something I do not need, or indeed something that would make me unhappy? God knows what He is doing. He grants those requests which in His better judgment ought to be granted. My gifts do not include knowing His plans for the future, nor do they include always knowing the best requests to make.

I do need to pray, and I do pray; despite the emphasis on petition (the very word "pray" is a verb for making a request, and several of the Greek words we understand that way have that root sense) the core of prayer is getting to know God. I don't mind when my sons come ask me for money, but I also want them to take time to tell me what is happening in their lives, their jobs, their relationships, their hobbies. I want them to be interested in what I am doing as well. So I converse with God, and tell him my worries. I figure it's up to Him to decide what to do about them; He is, after all, smarter than I am.

Hardship

Some would look at my life and question why I believe. If I believe in God, should He, if He is real, not reward me with the comforts of life, the prosperity promised to Abraham and so many others in the Bible? I cite my own experience as evidence that supports my own belief, but that experience does not seem to include what looks on the outside to be a comfortable and prosperous worry-free life. Why do I persist?

There are wealthy Christians in the world. I have never been one of them. I remember working in Christian broadcasting, listening to some of the wealthiest Christian teachers in the world ask audiences to send more money to support their work, while I was applying for food stamps and heating assistance because the barely-above-minimum-wage broadcasting job did not keep us out of poverty. I have always driven old cars (I have always lived where cars are a necessity, as it is miles to the store, and that's where the public transportation passes), cars which are falling apart despite my meager efforts to hold them together, never having enough money for proper regular maintenance, always fighting with utility companies to keep the heat, or the electric, or the water on for a few days, sometimes driving without legally required insurance because there was no money to pay for it. I have also seen hopes and dreams dashed, opportunities that were expected to turn the tide dissolving to nothing, open doors slamming in my face. The question might be raised, if God does not meet my needs, provide for me what life requires, even give me the opportunity to earn a decent income, why do I not give up my faith in Him?

Let me not misrepresent my situation. We have, as far as I recall, never gone hungry. We have made some rather strange and unexpected meals from whatever remained in the pantry before more food arrived. There have been times when we could loosen our belts a bit, catch up on the back bills, replace a dead car with another used one, even help our kids with their bills. Sometimes they have helped us with ours, as have our parents at times. As I said, though, I am not rich; I am probably, in financial terms, very poor.

Nor am I the only impoverished Christian in the world. For many of us, when we read the psalmist's words, "I've never seen the righteous forsaken nor his seed begging bread,"[140] we're tempted to say, "You're not looking hard enough." I have had a hard life not particularly marked by great successes. Many other believers have had the same. If this religion is not delivering success, why do I not abandon it in favor of something that works?

That is a very shallow view. I do not embrace Christianity because I expect it to provide benefits to me, now or ever. I embrace it because I am persuaded it is true. It happens to promise eternal benefits of some sort. Yet if the truth promised eternal misery, and was clearly the truth, the honest person would accept it, embrace it as the truth. Many atheists accept what they think is the truth about death, that once life ends it is over. It is not what they would want to believe; they believe it because they are persuaded it is true.[141] In the same way, I am persuaded that Christianity is true, and if I

---

[140] Psalm 37:25, from memory.

get no benefits from it at all ever, as an honest person I must still accept whatever fate it holds. That it happens to be optimistic about the eternal future is a fact about it. That it gives no guarantees about the present life is another.

Further, if someone told you that Christianity was about God's provision of comfort, he was at best badly mistaken. God's interest is in the production of character. The epistles speak much of how suffering produces endurance (Paul and James both say this),[142] which is viewed as a positive character trait.[143]

Besides, the Book of Job answered this for us, when Satan was visiting God's court and God pointed to the example of Job: of course someone experiencing all the blessings God can give will honor God for it. Christianity is criticized because there are wealthy Christians who luxuriate in their riches; is it also to be criticized because there are impoverished believers struggling in life? Had I come to this book and said that I believe in God

---

[141] Arguably there are some atheists who want death to be the end, because that excuses them from any obligation in life. If there is no afterlife the only consequences for our actions are those incurred in this life, and thus those who are rich and/or powerful enough can misbehave with impunity, knowing that they will probably avoid any retribution. Belief in an afterlife raises questions concerning life now, and whether we ought to be acting in a way that will prepare us for something later. Yet it must be accepted that not all atheists hold their belief for this reason.

[142] Paul in Romans 5:3, James in James 1:3.

[143] Friedrich Nietzsche is often quoted for his statement, "That which does not kill us makes us stronger," but the New Testament beat him to it with "suffering produces endurance", and in fact arguably says that that which does kill us also makes us stronger.

because He has given me everything in life anyone could want, you might well respond that I foolishly think God has made me rich and that's why I believe. Yet God has not made me rich, and still I believe. I consider the evidence for God to be strong enough that my own circumstances do not contradict it.

Obvious

I have not, I suspect, proved beyond a reasonable doubt to all my readers that God exists, or that Jesus Christ is God manifest as a man. I think that I have provided what in law would be called clear and convincing proof, but perhaps it is only the preponderance of the evidence. Perhaps the skeptical reader at this point thinks that the evidence is insufficient for the claim, that is, that if God really exists, it ought to be more obvious, that people should be able to see that He does indeed exist without any possibility of doubt. After all, if God exists, that fact requires a major reassessment of everything else we believe and everything we do. John Calvin put it well:

> For how can the idea of God enter your mind without instantly giving rise to the thought, that since you are his workmanship, you are bound, by the very law of creation, to submit to his authority?—that your life is due to him?—that whatever you do ought to have reference to him? If so, it undoubtedly follows that your life is sadly corrupted, if it is not framed in obedience to him, since his will ought to be the law of our lives.[144]

Given that as the price of believing in God, should it not be the kind of fact that can be proved unquestionably? Why does God not make His existence completely obvious, if He expects us to believe it?

---

[144] John Calvin, *Institutes of the Christian Religion*, Book 1, Chapter 2, §2.

Some would say no. Given a cost/benefit analysis of the Christian message, if there is so much as an articulable suspicion that it might be true, the rational choice is to embrace it.[145] If it is true the ultimate outcome of everything in your life hangs on that decision; if it is false, it does not much matter either way.[146] On the other hand, an honest man does not profess beliefs he does not actually think to be true, and Christianity encourages its adherents to be honest. The only reason to become a Christian is that you have concluded it to be at least more likely true than false, and the greater the level of certainty, the more reasonable such a profession is. So why does God allow there to be a doubt, any possibility of an alternative conclusion?

This, of course, is seeing it from our perspective; if God created us, we can only understand our own existence by seeing it from His perspective. After all, He must have had a reason to create us, and that by default becomes our reason for existing, and the reason for the way the world is. It seems likely that He made it right, and that this means that the level of possible doubt of His existence is a necessary part of the design to meet the purpose. We thus can only understand the design if we know the purpose.

---

[145] The suggestion is made that it is better to believe in the giant flying spaghetti monster because it might exist and the consequences of unbelief are serious. The flaw here is that there is not even the slightest hint that such a creature might exist. For the existence of God one might argue that the evidence is inadequate to support the belief, but it cannot be said to be non-existent.

[146] This is known as Pascal's Wager, first articulated by Blaise Pascal.

We might imagine that the creation of the
universe was an accident, that one day God (or some
lesser spirit being, as the Gnostics have it) made a
mistake, and the universe popped into existence. Or
perhaps the universe is by metaphor a sandcastle on
the beach, that God took great care in building it just
so he could look at it, and perhaps watch it be
destroyed by the tides (this is the way the Deists saw
it, absent the sense of entropy). However, the Bible
gives us a different view. It is clear from the
beginning that God had a purpose in creating, and
from the arrival of Jesus that that purpose involved
His love for people. From the calling of Abraham
forward, it is evident that God wanted people He
could call His own. That notion unfolds through the
text until we see that God wanted something
analogous to children.

We are given an image of God whose identity is
complex in a way that might be analogous to the
difference between triangles (personality as we
understand it) and pyramids (personality as it
applies to God).[147]   It is explained, somewhat
loosely, as one being in three persons. Theologians
spend thousands of pages trying to grasp the
relationships between them and how that actually
works, but it is clear that it has always been that
way, that before there was a universe, before there
was time as we understand it, there was God as what
we call Father, Son, and Holy Spirit. These three
are one, and yet they are also distinct; and they live
in a relationship characterized by love. God
understood that love is good, and He wanted there to

---

[147] This metaphor is adapted from C. S. Lewis, who in *Beyond
Personality*, op cit., used squares and cubes; I thought triangles
and pyramids more appropriate, although still imperfect.

be more love; but for there to be more love, there must somehow be more persons to share that love. He created the world so that He could create people, so that He could develop something like children who would love Him and each other. That was the best way He could find to increase how much love there is.[148]

That means that we exist to learn to love and trust Him. We do this in part by learning to love others, which is where the risk is; we express our love for God in large part by showing our trust in Him.

This purpose, though, creates a complication. God presumably could have created us, appeared before us in unchallengeable power, and announced that He had made us to love Him. We then would acquiesce to the demand, and act as if we loved Him; yet most of us would not really love Him, but would simply recognize that it is in our own best interests to appease the powerful being who claims to be God.[149]

---

[148] It is important to bear in mind both that the parent/child process is ultimately only a metaphor for the relationships between God and Christ and between God and us, and at the same time that it is a process God created specifically to be such a metaphor and thus is in some ways more like a two-dimensional drawing of a three-dimensional object. It does not tell the entire story, but it tells more than most metaphors.

[149] Arguably this is what He did in the Exodus account, appearing dramatically to the Israelites after demonstrating His power in the plagues against Egypt and the deliverance from their oppressors, leading them across the Red Sea, and speaking from Mount Sinai. Equally arguably, the consequence was not that they loved Him but that they feared Him. It might be objected that He should have known this would be the outcome, but indeed He undoubtedly did know, and did it so that we, too, would know that that approach does

Therein lie the twin problems. On the one hand, no matter what proofs God were to display, we could always question whether He was indeed God, our creator, or some pretender of immense power trying to trick us into a position of vulnerability. On the other hand, the fact that He is God is not sufficient for us to love and trust Him; He has to prove that He is trustworthy, and earn our love.

The Bible thus gives us a history of God's dealings with men, in which He carefully over time demonstrates that He is, in fact, that God who made us, that He seeks a relationship with us built on love and trust, and that for that to happen we have to learn to be loving and loveable, trustworthy and trusting, in a word, *good*. We see the process in microcosm in the life of Abraham, as God introduces Himself to the patriarch first by saying in essence, "If you'll trust me enough to leave this home, I will take you to a better one." As their relationship develops, God discusses His plans to punish the wicked people of Sodom and Gomorrah, taking Abraham's opinion into account and so saving the family of Abraham's nephew Lot. Then God promises to give Abraham children, and to do so through his first wife Sarah; God proves Himself by fulfilling that promise. He then asks Abraham to trust Him enough to put that first and only child, Isaac, through whom all of God's other promises were to be fulfilled, on an altar. Abraham did so, and God intervened, and we see that they had come to a place where they fully trusted each other. That was the prototype of the relationship God wanted to have with each of us, in which we each fully trust

---

not work.

Him and He in turn knows that He can fully trust each of us.[150]

His actions through the Bible echo this pattern. He demonstrates to Israel that they can trust Him, and asks them to prove that He can trust them. They fail; He responds to bring them back to Himself, sometimes through punishment, sometimes through forgiveness. Some of them grasp it; some reject Him.

Finally He sets the stage for His own arrival—a stage in which Israel is ready to do what must be done, and in which the world is ready for the message to reach more civilizations than ever before.[151]   He arrived and demonstrated in His teaching and His actions how to act and how to love —which prove to be the same thing. Then after He

---

[150] This aspect of the trust relationship God wants with each of us is presented more fully in the author's book *Do You Trust Me?*

[151] Although the account known as Acts of the Apostles focuses on the transmission of the message through the Roman Empire as far as Rome, it is evident even from its own text that much was happening outside that part. We see Barnabas separate from Paul and head somewhere else; we see most of the Apostles, along with early Christians, driven from Judea by persecution after the stoning of Steven. There is some evidence that Thomas preached through a substantial part of India, and that either he or Bartholomew may have reached China; there is also strong evidence of diplomatic relations, and thus communication, between Rome and China. The "barbaric" areas of Germany and England were also reached by missionary work, and we have early translations of the New Testament in Ethiopic, carrying the influence south into Africa. There were certainly parts of the world that would not be reached for centuries, but this was the first time in history that ideas could be disseminated over many cultures and countries relatively quickly. It was in that sense the right time to send a message to the entire world.

died, He returned and sent people into the world to let everyone know what He had done, and that God was waiting to receive us, forgive us, and make us His children.

This also provides a reason why God might have created a universe which appeared different from its reality—that is, for example, one that was only a few thousand years old but appeared to be far older (if that is in fact what he did). If ultimately there is no possible alternative explanation for the existence and form of the universe than that God made it in six days, believing otherwise becomes irrational, and having faith in God is not a matter of trusting Him but of having no other rational option. Thus if God wants us to come to trust Him, there must always be a view of the universe which is at least viable as an alternative.

Ask

Ultimately, the proof that God exists is that you can meet Him. If you ask Him to demonstrate His existence to you, He will. However, there are two stories that I should add here.

A man had a job interview; he needed the job. When he reached the block where the office was, it was packed—not a single parking space in view. He made the right at the corner and started around the block, and as he was coming back to the starting point he still had not found a spot. He prayed. He said, "God, I really need to be on time for this interview, and would be so grateful if you could find me a parking place."   Then just as he was approaching the front door of the building, a car pulled into traffic, leaving an open space as close to the entrance as any could be, and he pulled into it. "Never mind, God," he said. "I found one myself."

The second story you can find in Luke 16:19ff. It is the story of the rich man and Lazarus. You can read it there.   What matters is that when the rich man begs that someone be sent back from the dead to warn his family and friends so that they would not suffer the same fate he did, Abraham, in the story, answers that if they do not believe Moses and the prophets, they will not believe even if someone rises from the dead.

It is an interesting note that in John 11 Jesus did bring someone back from the dead, whose name (perhaps not coincidentally) was Lazarus, although he was not a poor beggar as the character in the parable.   After that, Jesus Himself rose from the dead, and was seen by over five hundred witnesses. You do not believe, even though someone rose from the dead. That's perhaps forgivable; you did not get to cross-examine those witnesses yourself and don't trust the records of their testimony. Yet if you ask Jesus to prove Himself to you, be mindful that it is simple enough to ignore the proof, to explain the miraculous and tell yourself it does not prove anything. In the end, you have to face the question of whether for you any proof would be sufficient, or whether your own stubbornness is great enough that a bodily visitation by Jesus Himself would be discounted as a sensory hallucination requiring a trip to the psychiatric hospital. If no evidence could possibly be sufficient, you cannot complain that there is insufficient evidence. Nor can you complain if God, knowing that you will reject whatever evidence you see, will not waste effort sending you miracles for you to ignore.

So be honest with God and with yourself, and either ask Jesus to prove Himself and accept that what happens might be that proof, or don't bother asking if you are going to ignore the answer. Do not be dishonest, though: if you have decided that you could never believe in God on any amount of proof, recognize that it is not the foolishness of others that causes them to believe, but your own choice that causes you to disbelieve.

Conclusions

I admit that there are questions that I cannot answer about God and Christ and the Christian faith; I have shown that there are equally questions that cannot be answered about the universe without reference to him. Sartre himself admitted that his greatest philosophical problem was why is there something rather than nothing, which means in essence that this icon of modern existential philosophy was unable to overcome Aquinas' cosmological argument: that the very existence of the universe means that something must cause it, and with the more recent recognition of entropy[152] we are even more assured that the universe is not eternally pre-existent.   Famed twentieth century atheist Antony Flew in his last years at the dawn of the twenty-first century was persuaded to Deism (or at least theism) by teleology, when confronted with the complexity of DNA, and thus the question of how something so complicated as we are (fearfully and wonderfully made) stands between us and atheism.   Why do all men everywhere share very similar, even identical, notions of a universal moral code, which often goes against our own self-interest, often against our own drives, sometimes against our family, tribal, or national interests, sometimes even against our reason, yet insists on our conformity while leaving us powerless to conform? Could it be that entirely random sequences of events have created an organ within ourselves which itself works by what must be random electrochemical events yet produces something we call reason and trust to

---

[152] More recent, that is, than Aquinas; Sartre was certainly aware of entropy.

deliver a true and correct understanding of reality? These are questions that have never been adequately answered without reference to some kind of God. There might be questions concerning my faith I cannot answer even yet, and some I might never be able to answer (unlike so many others, I do not see heaven as the place where we discover who was right and what all the right answers were, but the place where we discover that it never mattered so much as we supposed), but Christians are not alone with unanswerable questions.

Billions over centuries have attested that God is alive, that they have encountered Him, in essence met Him. You can ignore that testimonial evidence only by asserting that those people were mistaken; yet many of them, from the Apostles to Saint Teresa of Calcutta, changed the world in positive ways because of what you claim is a mistake. You can stand on the belief that God must not exist because you have not met Him, but that would be a poor basis to disbelieve claims of the existence of any human whose existence is claimed by others. You think you have not seen evidence for the existence of God when in actuality you have seen much, and discounted it all as insufficient. If you will not be persuaded by any amount of evidence, there is no point in discussing the evidence. If you will not give Jesus an honest chance to prove His own godhood, you are dishonest in asserting that He cannot be God. In the end, you are basing your investigation on your conclusion, skewing the data to meet the desired result. You condemn corporations and governments for such tactics, but freely use them to protect yourself from facing the most demanding challenge to your understanding of reality and your claim to self-determination you could face. God is still God, and Jesus Christ is the one He sent. The proof is there. Go ahead and ask for confirmation, but don't be dishonest about it.

In the end, it's up to you to look, or you will never see.

Appendix: Sent to Hell?

In discussing the notion of being sent to hell, I recalled having addressed the question from a slightly different perspective not too many months previously. In editing this book it seemed that this other perspective might also be helpful, but did not fit well in the text at that point, so I decided to insert it as an appendix here and footnote it there.

The frequent attack to which I was at that point responding insists that it would be a cruel God who condemns people to an eternity of suffering for failure to believe. I think this is entirely wrong. Certainly it is not entirely the fault of those who make this claim that they have it wrong, as there are Christians who would agree with the statement on its face. I think, though, that this view is backwards, and I'd like to suggest something of a parable to put it right.

We are all living on the Titanic, and it is sinking. Of course, it is sinking very slowly, so slowly in fact that most of us never notice it. The orchestra is still playing, they're serving lobster for lunch, and the crew is assuring everyone that everything is under control. The captain himself is reminding people that the ship cannot sink, and telling us that whatever the voices of Nervous Nellies are saying we should ignore them and enjoy the cruise. Oh, yes, and ignore that flying saucer that has settled above us.

I forgot to mention that part. While the ship is sinking, this flying saucer has arrived and is hovering above it. It has dropped a lot of ropes with hooks on the ends. Better to ignore them, we are told. The aliens are obviously fishing for humans they can catch. Of those few voices who insist the ship is sinking, some are saying that these are not fishing lines but lifelines, and we need to trust that the aliens are here to rescue us, and will take us to safety, if we simply connect ourselves to one of the lines. They do so, and continue to encourage others to do so. On the other hand, it is a flying saucer; who can know what the aliens really intend?

We could push this story a bit further, taking a trope from *Starman*:[153] someone appears on the ship who claims to be one of the aliens, but who took the form of the passengers and crew so that we wouldn't be, well, alienated. He persuades more people to connect to the hooks. The crew, and those passengers who do not want to believe the ship is sinking, are upset with him, and ultimately throw him overboard. People think that that's the end; a few stand near the rail watching the spot where he hit the water. They are the only ones who see when a line descends from the flying saucer to that spot, and hauls him to the ship. Yet they tell others that they saw it, that the one who claimed to be an alien was taken to the flying saucer after being thrown into the ocean.

All of which is to say that God does not, it seems to me, condemn anyone to an eternity of torment for any reason. Rather, we have so condemned ourselves. He offers to deliver us from our self-imposed punishment. We just have to trust Him. If we don't trust Him, we probably don't believe even

---

[153] 1984 John Carpenter film from Sony Pictures in which an alien crashes on earth, creates a human body for itself, and interacts with humanity while trying to rendezvous with a rescue vessel.

that there is any danger from which we need to be delivered; we'll simply go down with the ship. If we don't trust Him, then even if we do believe that the ship is sinking we may think that it's better to die in the pain we can foresee than to allow ourselves to be taken by aliens whose motives we cannot fathom. It is not, in the end, about God condemning anyone for not believing, but about God rescuing anyone who will trust Him and grab the lifeline.

To change the image slightly, the world is a train hurtling toward some destination unknown to us. One of us, one of the passengers, changed the destination, such that we are headed for a terrible collision and conflagration. God is offering to pull people off the train who are willing to trust Him to do so. To choose not to accept that offer is to choose to die in the crash—or, abandoning the metaphor, not choosing to trust Christ for salvation is choosing the default alternative, to spend eternity in hell, excluded from the joy of heaven.

Appendix: Dualism?

Years ago I was involved in a correspondence with an intellectual Buddhist, and he asked me about "dualism". Our discussion immediately derailed, because I had only ever used that word in one sense, and he was using it in another completely unrelated sense. For the sake of clarity, I will address his meaning first.

The word "dualism" is sometimes used for the belief that there is a dichotomy between a spirit world and a material world, usually identifying the spirit world with all that is good and perfect and the material world with all that is corrupt and evil. This idea is strongly embraced in Gnosticism, deriving from Plato's conception of a world of ideals in which exists the perfect cube and the perfect sphere, in contrast to the material world in which all such shapes are imperfect and in which decay increases the imperfection over time.

I certainly agree that there is such a dichotomy, a material world and a distinct spirit world. It is one of the points that make people such amazing creations, that in creating them God somehow connected a spirit to a lump of matter.[154] However, I do not find that everything spiritual is good, nor that everything material is evil. I strongly reject the notion that all our wickedness arises from the fact that we have material bodies—I think our spirits are capable of quite a bit of wickedness that has no relation to our physical existences. However, I don't know how much of this is relevant to any of the questions posed by this book concerning the

---

[154] It may be that animals are similar in this regard; that is uncertain but not relevant to the present issue.

existence of God. If God exists in any of the forms
we usually imagine, there is a spirit world of some
sort, and the material world is in some way or sense
separate from it. If that is all that is meant by
"dualism" in this context, there is little more to say
about it.

Some deny this concept. The more ancient
denial is that the material world does not exist but is
an illusion within the realm of the spirit world, and
that we become more spiritual by distancing
ourselves from all things material, generally by
ascetic practices. I do not think the world is an
illusion; I do not think most people today are likely
to believe that. However, no one who believes that
the material world does not exist disbelieves in a
spirit world with some concept of a god or gods.

The modern denial is materialism, that there is
no spirit world. That is a matter I think is addressed
throughout this book, and if we conclude that God
exists then there is at least one spirit and must be, in
our way of perceiving realities, something analogous
to a place for that spirit to be.

However, the sort of dualism with which I was
then more familiar is that of "Yin/Yang", the notion
that there are co-equal opposite powers of light and
darkness, good and evil. Although this is a popular
view, it has a number of serious flaws.

One problem is that on careful examination,
"evil" does not seem actually to be its own thing.
"Good" is independent; "evil" is derivative. Good
could exist entirely without evil; evil could not exist
without good.

Part of that is that there is nothing that is both
evil and desirable. We think there is, but actually

everything that people want that is evil is a corruption of something that is good. Sex is not evil; sex is a rightly desirable good that is perverted into something distorted into evil by selfishness. Wealth is not evil; greed is evil, as it seeks wealth to the detriment of other people. People do evil acts to obtain good objects—frequently in unfair proportions, but still good. No one wants evil for the sake of evil. It does not really exist as its own thing, and thus cannot be the co-equal opposite of good.

However, were we to suppose that it were, we would hit a more serious problem. If we have a good god and an evil god, and they are equal to each other, then good and evil themselves are equal— equally valuable, equally appropriate, equally right. We in the main happen to prefer the good, but that becomes our personal preference. We recognized in connection with the moral argument for the existence of God that if God did not exist then "good" was simply a personal preference. That becomes even more the case if there are two co-equal opposite gods, one good and one evil: our preference for the good is nothing more than our preference, and we have no right to condemn anyone who chooses to prefer the evil god. Building a hospital and bombing an office building become acts of effectively equal value, without moral import. Good is only morally better than evil if it is based on a supreme God who is good; if it is based on one of two co-equal gods of whom the other is evil, then good is only morally equal to evil, and cannot act against evil while remaining good. Only if good is morally superior to evil at the divine level can it be morally justified in opposing evil in the material world.

So this popular dualism breaks down under scrutiny. Either the God above all gods is good, or good is only a name we give to that which we prefer. If it is only that which we prefer, then by its own standards we are unable to condemn those who prefer evil, as it is, as discussed earlier, only a personal preference.

There is one other sort of dualism popular in pagan religions, that of the distinction between the god and the goddess. I find this to be an unnecessary appeal to feminism which ultimately creates division and inequality rather than the equality it is meant to foster.

In the Genesis account of creation, we are told that God made man in His own image. We are then told that in forming woman, God took something out of man and formed it into woman, and that the reason this was done was in part so that God could take the two separated parts and reunite them as one creature. Thus it is man and woman together who form the complete image of God.

What we mostly miss in this is that the first statement must mean that God made an androgynous human creature in His own image, because God contains within Himself all that is masculine and all that is feminine, all that is male and all that is female. In creating woman He took part of that image of Himself away from the man and formed it into the woman. Yet at the divine level, that division does not exist; God is the entirety of all that is man and all that is woman conjoined.

What the god and goddess concept does is make that division fundamental, essential. It means that maleness and femaleness are irreconcilable concepts, that the two can never be truly united. It also means that there is an eternal tension between them, as if men and women are fighting for control of the universe on behalf of the god and goddess on whom they were separately modeled.

We again have the problem of co-equal opposites, although in this case it is really about a war of the sexes, a battle over which gender controls all, and a recognition that neither can win yet they must remain at odds, separate. The unity of marriage cannot be found in this concept, because at the divine level they are irreconcilable.

Only a concept of one supreme good God provides the foundation for the world as we perceive it.

Appendix: Encore?

At the beginning of this book I mentioned someone who is in large part the impetus for my motivation to write it, someone who complained that the fact that I believe is a problem for his agnosticism. As I was reading through what was the fourth draft, I realized that he had a second issue which I did not address directly, and which on the one hand does not really fit into the book while on the other hand is as much a part of the same objection as to require discussing. He wanted to know why God did not treat him as he treated others, that is, particular others, those to whom God revealed himself dramatically. God visited Abraham in bodily form, spoke to Moses from a bush that was alight but not burning, sent angels to Gideon and dreams to Joseph. My friend has had no such experience. He asserts that he would certainly believe, if God treated him as he treated them. Why is it, if God can perform these miraculous undeniable manifestations, He does not do them for us today?

On consideration, though, we have answered it; we just have not answered it directly, mentioning reasons along the way without referring to the fact that this was a separate question. So some of this is recapitulating what has already been said, putting it into the context of the question of why God does not treat each of us as He treated the heroes of the Bible.

If something appeared before you which seemed to be an angel, how could you be certain that it was what it claimed to be? "If they will not believe Moses and the Prophets, they will not believe even if someone were to rise from the dead,"[155] Jesus said, and proved that, too, in his own resurrection. As C. S. Lewis observed in recounting the story of the one person he knew who actually saw a ghost,[156] seeing is not believing, and believing has much control over what we think we see. Agnostics and atheists argue all the time that believers are prone to see what they expect, but that argument cuts both ways: those who disbelieve are prone to ignore what contradicts their disbelief, also seeing what they expect instead of what exists. Were God to appear to my friend as an angel or a supernatural manifestation of some sort, there is no guarantee that he would be unable to find some explanation for it; and, as we commented, a compelling proof of the existence of God would be counter-productive to God's purpose, as our motivation for acting lovingly would not be love for God and others but fear for the consequences of the alternative. We become as drivers who obey the traffic laws not because we are good drivers who believe they promote safety and save lives, but because we know that the police are out in force distributing citations to all violators.

It is also the case (as Lewis also somewhere said) that given the infinite creativity of our Creator, the prayer least likely to be answered is "Encore", that is, having done something he is unlikely to do it again.[157] It is not impossible; Elijah called fire from above at least thrice, and it had previously fallen in

---

[155] Luke 16:31, author's paraphrase.

[156] In the opening of *Miracles: A Preliminary Study, op. cit.* The story was that the woman in question did not believe in ghosts either before or after the event, and so sought a natural psychological explanation for the apparition. The point thus is that what we see does not prove that which we will not accept under any condition.

the temple when Solomon consecrated the new altar. However, only Noah faced a flood, only Moses had a burning bush, only Elijah was taken in a whirlwind. One of the marks of an encounter with God may well be that it is uniquely tailored to the individual experiencing it. To ask to have the same experience as some other person is in a sense to ask to be not yourself but him. The events in your life are intended for you.

Does this mean that God treats us inequitably? Not at all—it means He treats us individually. Were I to buy a guitar amp as a present for my fourth son, he would be pleased and would immediately put it to good use; the same gift for my second son would be puzzling and of no value, because he has never, to this point, shown any interest in learning to play the guitar. Certainly it is apparent that making a "favorite dinner" for each of my five sons would involve making five different dinners. They have different tastes. They also have different hopes, and different fears, different abilities and different flaws. To treat different people equally, it is necessary to treat them differently. Even in our justice system we recognize this, providing free attorneys for indigent defendants, and translators for those who do not speak our common language well, in the name of equal protection.

---

[157] In an article about legendary rock guitarist Eric Clapton a writer admitted to wondering whether the slower quieter largely acoustic style of later music was because the elderly musician had himself started losing ability with age. Sitting in on a private jam session persuaded him otherwise, so he asked why, if the guitarist could still play like that, he did not do so in his newer releases. Clapton's answer, reportedly, was, "I already did that." We thus see that even creative humans try to avoid repeating themselves.

It must also be noted that every time God spoke to someone in the Bible, it was because He had something for him to do, and the more evident He made it that this was His directive, the more difficult and dangerous the task required was going to be. We see this quite clearly in the account of Gideon facing the Midianites.[158] God provided proof upon proof, from an angel calling fire to consume a sacrifice to miracles of dew on or not on a fleece, and when Gideon was absolutely confidently able to say that with God on his side it did not matter that he had only thirty thousand volunteers against the one hundred twenty thousand professional Midianite soldiers, God said that he was going to do it with three hundred men instead. The more God does to persuade you that He is talking to you, the bigger appears the risk you face in doing what you are told.

The opposite side of that is also true: if God knows that no amount of proof will be adequate to persuade you, He will not waste His effort. If you truly have never seen any evidence of the existence of God, and none of what is said in this book strikes you as meaningful in that regard, then perhaps you should be asking yourself what evidence would be sufficient, and whether you would be willing to conform your life to the new information if you received it. When the psalmist wrote, "The fool has said in his heart, 'There is no God,'"[159] he did not mean that fools are all atheists nor that atheists are all fools. No one at that time would have asserted that there were no gods. He meant that there were people who acted as if God were irrelevant to their daily lives. As we have seen, the question matters;

---

[158] Judges 6f.
[159] Psalm 14:1, 53:1, author's rendering.

what we believe about eternal things will impact what we think and do about temporal ones. Yet an intellectual assent to the fact that God exists (which is what proof ultimately creates) is not the same thing as an honest trust that what God directs is the best course in life. To say that we believe in God is either to say that we give Him the right to rule our lives, or to say that we are in rebellion against the Lawful Ruler of the universe. God is looking for people who will trust Him and obey Him, not people who will assent to His existence and ignore it.

My friend would at this point say that if he had certain proof of God's existence, in the form of some undeniably supernatural manifestation, he would certainly be willing to do whatever God directed, and to trust God. The evidence suggests otherwise. When Moses was standing in front of the bush that was not burning he argued that God had chosen the wrong man. Although Gideon had already seen the miraculous several times, God still had to reassure him before that final battle. Yet the evidence also suggests this: God has given you enough proof of His existence and His trustworthiness for you to believe and trust Him enough for what He is asking you to do now.

It is also the case that for most of those to whom God spoke, they did not learn to trust Him by seeing miraculous manifestations, but by obeying what they were told and learning that He would come through for them. Moses did not trust God simply because he saw the bush that was not burning, nor even because God worked miracles against Egypt. He came to trust God because God brought them to a place where they could leave, and because when God led them to the edge of the water God parted the water for them to cross, and because when they were in the dry wilderness God provided food and water for the multitude. It was because obedience involved taking a risk, and God met him at the point of the danger.

It thus appears that to the degree that you trust God, He will show Himself to you. He has given you enough evidence to begin, to believe that He is there and that He rewards those who trust Him. If you want more proof, you should act on the proof you already have.

Find more books from this author at
dimensionfold.com/authors/mark-joseph-young/